THINGS ONLY MEN KNOW

PRESTON GILLHAM

HARVEST HOUSE PUBLISHERS
Eugene, Oregon 97402

Cover by Terry Dugan Design, Minneapolis, Minnesota
Back cover photo by Smiley Irvin

THINGS ONLY MEN KNOW

Copyright © 1999 by Preston Gillham
Published by Harvest House Publishers
Eugene, Oregon 97402

Library of Congress Cataloging-in-Publication Data
Gillham, Preston H.
    Things only men know / Preston Gillham.
        p.   cm.
    ISBN 1-56507-430-0
    1. Masculinity—Religious aspects—Christianity. 2. Men (Christian theology) 3. Men—United
States—Religious life. I. Title.
BV4597.G455   1999
248.8'42—DC21   98-46661
                                                                                                      CIP

Printed in the United States of America

99   00   01   02   03   / BP /   10   9   8   7   6   5   4   3   2   1

For my dad, **Dr. Bill Gillham**, who charted my course toward manhood and shared with me things only men know

and

for my SWAT buddies, men who are always on the road to victory. In order around the conference room table: **Max Falls, Kent Riley, Lamar Smith, Walter Williams, Dan Bates, John Ott, Jeff Harp, Jeff Moore,** and for the man who hosts us each week, **Scott Walker.**

Acknowledgements

Winston Churchill said, "Writing a book is an adventure. To begin with, it is a toy and an amusement. Then it becomes a master, then it becomes a tyrant. The last phase is that just as you are about to be reconciled to your servitude, you kill the monster and fling him about to the public."

Seriously, I have enjoyed every minute, but I am glad this book is out of my hands and into yours. As is the case with any project, its completion and success must be attributed to more than my hard work.

Bob Hawkins, Jr. and Harvest House Publishers: Bob, thank you and your fine staff for pursuing me and not giving up on me or what you believed was possible.

Jerry "Chip" MacGregor: Chip, your wisdom, counsel, and red marks revolutionized the original manuscript and helped transform it into a book. I treasure our friendship and the honor of working with you as both my editor and friend. Thank you for helping me articulate what God put on my heart.

Larry Worden: Larry, thanks for your work to compile my reference notes. You will never know how helpful your efforts were.

Dr. Fred Tomaselli and The Fold Family Ministries: Lots of words have hit the page since I began outlining in the corner room above the counseling center at The Fold. If you look closely between the lines, you can see a sorrel and a dapple-gray horse cantering into a fresh Vermont snow below my window, inspiring the paragraphs on these pages.

Dr. Bob Langston: Doc Bob, the Lazy H holds a special place in my heart. The smells, the sights, the memories all rushed back at me each time I looked up from my writing at the kitchen table in your farm house. Thank you for making the Lazy H available for me to retreat and write.

Caryn Walker: Caryn, thank you for assisting me in getting the final details of the manuscript together. In addition, your thoughts after reading the rough draft were invaluable. Not only are you a tremendous contributor to the team at Lifetime Guarantee, you are a wonderful example of Christ's life.

The SWAT Team: What more could a man ask than to be surrounded with men of your stature and integrity? I prayed and asked God for close friends and He delivered beyond my wildest dreams. I appreciate you, I admire you, I value you as my friends, I respect you as strong men.

Dianne: Sweetheart, I've told you time and again how much your support, encouragement, and prayer have meant to me, but now, here it is in writing. Thank you for standing by me, for being understanding when my mind was engrossed in writing and it was supposed to be elsewhere. Thank you for throwing the party when I signed the contract with Harvest House. You are a great wife and a tremendous friend. Life would not have the same luster if you were not part of it. I love you.

John Lyly said, "Look in thy heart and write." To the best of my ability, I have looked into my heart and trusted the Lord to reveal His heart through mine in these pages. In a sense, you hold my heart—and I trust His as well—in your hands. That is what writing and reading is all about. God bless you as you consider the things only men know.

Preston Gillham
Fort Worth, Texas

Contents

SETTING THE CORNER POST

The pickup bed was full of hard work and it was going to be a hot day. We had two long-handled shovels, one sharp-shooter, two post hole diggers, a five-foot iron bar for busting rock, a pick, a sledge, six bags of Portland cement, a wheelbarrow, two hoes, a four-foot level, four two-by-sixes, some six-by-eight treated posts, and a chain saw. Cecil and I were building a fence, and today we were going to set the corner post.

There is an art to building a fence and every rancher takes pride in the ingenuity, repair, and appearance of his fences. The country usually dictates how a fence is done. For some, the art form is displayed in being able to build a fence where no man has built before. Just a few months ago I noticed an Arkansas rancher's fence running along a rocky ledge. It was impossible to drive posts into the rock ledge, so he filled old tires with cement and stuck a metal fence post in the middle of the cement. It wasn't pretty, but it was ingenious and it worked. For others, the art form is a fence running straight and true, with wire strands tight enough to twang like a banjo.

But whether the fence is built on the Lazy H in Arkansas, the XIT in Texas, the yard around the house in Atascadero, California,

or to keep the goats in Mrs. Millsap's pasture out of Mr. Sturte-
vant's orchard in Virginia, one thing is common about all good
fences: The corner post is anchored well.

We jostled along over the pasture road, flushing an occasional covey of quail, dodging a terrapin catching the sun on his
back, and watching the ground fog dissipate in the valley as the
sun rose over the stand of hardwoods to the east. If all went
according to plan, the majority of our digging would be done
before the heat began in earnest. But then, it doesn't seem to
matter what time of the year it is, digging post holes always generates a sweat.

Building a fence is like most things—preparation and attention to detail are essential if you intend to be proud of your work
when you are finished. We already knew where the fence was
supposed to run and had spent the better part of the day-before-
yesterday determining the exact spot for the corner post to be
set. It was time now for the real work to begin.

We dug three holes that formed a right angle, with the hole
for the corner post being the middle hole or vertex of the angle.
Each hole was about three times larger than the diameter of the
post and approximately three feet deep. The going was tough,
and I wished more than once for one of those augers that
attaches to the power take-off on a tractor. But with each wish I
was jarred back to reality by the post hole diggers hitting the
bottom of the deepening hole.

It didn't take long to need a break. Cecil and I worked well
together in that neither of us felt like we had to outdo the other. We
worked at about the same pace, and anticipated what the other
was planning and needing. We were partners. With each break,
we sat on the tailgate of the truck, replenished our fluids, and
assessed our progress. By 9:00 A.M. sweat was coming through
the back of my leather gloves.

Once the last hole was finished, we selected the largest
timber as the corner post, dragged it out of the truck, and

dropped it into its hole. The remaining two creosote posts were also dropped into their holes, then we stepped back to eye our work and launch the next phase of our project.

At that point, Cecil and I made a trip to the creek, each carrying a five-gallon feed bucket and our lunch sack. We sat under the low branches of a cottonwood and ate an early lunch before filling our buckets with creek water and returning to mix the cement. There is a trick to getting the cement just the right consistency, and that's where my friend Cecil excelled. My job was to pour the water while he stirred with the hoe. And with the practiced eye of a true connoisseur, Cecil finally pronounced the cement ready to pour into the holes.

A little cement, a few rocks. A little cement, a few rocks. Tamp it down with the iron bar to wedge the rocks into place and get rid of air pockets. Plumb the post with the level. More cement and rocks. The bar again. The level. "It needs to come toward you some, Cecil. There." The bar. More cement, more rock. One last check with the level and the rest of the cement. We would fill in with dirt later.

We repeated the same routine for the other two posts, finishing ahead of schedule, which meant there was time for a dip in the creek before heading back for the evening chores. Since there weren't any cattle in this pasture yet, we did not have to brace the posts. They would stay put and their footing could cure without being disturbed. We would be ready to tie the posts together and build the fence day-after-tomorrow.

This time of year, the weather doesn't vary much. In fact, two days later the news anchor was touting the "cool" front that pushed into the area overnight bringing with it a respite from the 98 degree heat that scorched us yesterday, and the day before, and the day before that as well. The day promised to be a delightful 92 degrees. I appreciated the weather man's optimism, and made a mental note to determine if I could feel the difference between 98 and 92 degrees while I was tangling with the barbed wire on the new fence.

The first order of the day was to get out of the truck and go pat the creosote timbers, push on them a little bit with the heel of our hands, bump them with our hips, and pronounce our earlier work a success. Celebrations, no matter how small, are important.

With Cecil on one end of a two-by-six and me on the other, we drove 20-penny, pole barn nails through the lumber and into the posts. This treated board, running parallel, four feet above the ground, and connecting the corner post to the side posts, would act to support the tops of the posts while the cement anchored the bottoms. Finally, we nailed a board diagonally from the corner post where the cross-members joined to the bottoms of the two side posts.

While I got the chain saw ready to run, Cecil measured the shortest post and marked the other two with a grease crayon to match its height. By that time, I had filled the chain saw's oil reservoir and gas tank and tightened the chain. I cut the tops off of the two taller posts and trimmed the two-by-sixes to length as Cecil followed behind, picking up the ends and tops and throwing them into the back of the truck. The corner post was anchored and set.

From this point, we would site off this corner post to where the other corner posts would be anchored and set the end of the fence row. Wire would be strung between the corner posts and pulled tight with the tractor. Intermediate posts would be driven every ten feet and the barbed wire would be fastened to them. And ending where we began—at a corner post—we would tie off our wire and complete our fencing project.

The corner post stands as a marker, is used as a site, pulled against with a tractor, and placed under constant tension. A good corner post is firmly anchored and makes a standard of excellence possible. It is anchored at the base and supported at the top.

A man is a lot like a corner post.

The Qualities of Men

The *story* of a man's life is the classic tale of a struggle between right and wrong, good and evil. He lives with constant tension, and how he conquers life and establishes himself proves if he truly understands masculinity or if he is misinformed about manhood.

Once the cattle are turned into the new pasture, they will test the fence, lean against the posts, and butt their heads against the timbers. A man's *strength* allows the world, his family, and his friends to push and pull against him. While everyone around him may test him, a strong man remains anchored in the rock at his feet and supported by the ties at his shoulders—other men.

Before a course can be plotted, there must be a starting point. A man was meant to site off, to gain your bearings from, to be a fixed object that brings sanity to the chaos swirling around life's pasture. A man is to be the *source* from which society gets its coordinates, the inspiration from which vision is spawned. If he is not, the world may as well get its bearings from the man in the moon.

The *significance* of a corner post is similar to the significance of a man. He is the marker of boundaries, the moral compass, the ethical benchmark. If a man is the source from which coordinates are derived, then his significance charts a heading for those around him to march toward. As a marker of boundaries, a man stands as that fixed point in which society finds security. If a man is anchored securely, his significance is indisputable and indispensable. If he is not, confusion reigns.

A man conveys *security*. He is an anchored point in a changing world. A man anchored firmly and supported above exudes dependability. His stance in life says, "I'm not going anywhere. Stand by me." On the other hand, there isn't anything quite so disheartening and disarming as a man who is not dependable. If he is not anchored as a corner post, those pushing and pulling against him feel him give, and without significant delay, insecurity takes root.

A man's *station* is a standard of excellence. You simply cannot have a shoddy corner post and hope to have a quality fence. A man stands, and those around him rally to his standard because a man's station requires him to live by his honor as protector, provider, warrior, and executor of the mantle of masculinity. This is manhood.

God takes as much pride in His fences as any earthly rancher does his. And if I am not mistaken, I hear He is setting corner posts today.

MEN ARE NO LONGER NECESSARY

Everything about a woman's body points to her role as a life-giver, nurturer, and care-provider, but a generation ago—almost two now—the proponents of the women's movement pushed the power of women and spoke of their abilities "to do what men do." They burned their bras and went without shirts, not to flaunt their breasts in sensuality, but to live and behave like men. They put forth the philosophy that men were not really necessary. One famous statement attributed to Gloria Steinem put it, "A woman needs a man like a fish needs a bicycle." Men were simply obstructions to get past en route to feminine fulfillment and the ultimate goal: equality.

Following the propaganda of Fonda, Steinem, and Brown, women sacrificed their traditional roles to push against the glass ceilings of corporate America. Their books, articles, and conquests filled the bookstores and media reports. They tossed out the book on how families function and rewrote it to suit their own philosophical ideologies. They began viewing men as the perpetrators of a vile and shameful prejudice against women. Men became bigots, and masculinity was synonymous with sexism, intolerance, and bias. Men were no longer the protectors and providers of society, women, and children; they were chauvinist pigs.

That message wormed its way into the hearts of women, who then passed it to their sons and daughters, who in turn passed it to the next generation. And now where are we? The books and propaganda in America's bookstores promoting feminism have been greatly reduced to make room for books concerning masculinity. Men are in crisis. They have been told for thirty years that masculinity is bad, sexist, and something to be fought against, tempered, sensitized, and overcome.

The masculine face is covered with a black bandana. Men feel robbed of their identities. If true masculinity is the man behind the mask, men feel obligated to protect society against this rogue-villain. In fact, men are torn: Should the mask be pulled off to discern the true identity, or should these shameful villains be hunted to extinction? A May 1998 *Newsweek* article on boys noted, "Even normal boy behavior has come to be considered pathological in the wake of the feminist movement."[1]

While there is a proliferation of books on masculinity, many of them talk primarily about what men *do,* and in the absence of male role models this is essential. But while it is important for us to understand what men do, more fundamentally we must understand who men *are.* How does a boy become a man? What makes a man masculine? How is manhood transferred from men to boys?

In response to the feminist movement, society has asked men to abdicate their masculinity and become more gentle, sensitive, and thoughtful. It is as though society is saying, "This is the modern era; you men are lagging behind. Masculinity is barbaric and uncivilized. What's with this hair all over your bodies? Brawn is out, consciousness is in. And we need to eliminate these noises and grunts you make instead of self-aware dialogue. Gritted-teeth determination is passé. Instead, focus on the tender sharing of your feelings. And by the way, romance is *en vogue,* not those passionate drives you exhibit. Really! Don't you think it is time you men get with the times?" As Robert Bly puts it in his seminal book *Iron John,* "The male in the past twenty years has become more thoughtful, more gentle. But by this process he has not become more free."[2]

Bly suggests a basic insecurity has developed in men. There is shame associated with being male. Masculinity is not OK, but something to be overcome en route to being more sensitive and thoughtful and—well, more *feminine.* Masculine energy is not welcome in western society. Testosterone is equated with primitive, wild, and uncivilized life. Again, Robert Bly says, "All the great cultures except ours preserve and have lived with images of this positive male energy."[3] Dr. James Dobson quotes a study by Dr. Charles Winick at City University of New York in which he analyzed more than two thousand cultures that have existed in world history. Winick found only fifty-five cultures in which masculinity and femininity were blurred. Not one of those unisexual societies survived for more than a few years.[4]

Differences Are a Good Thing

The fact that many men became proud and disdainful of "women's work" and the roles women play in society has certainly fueled the fires of the women's movement. This attitude among men is inexcusable. As Pastor Jack Hayford says, "If manhood is diminished, perverted, imbalanced, misunderstood, impotent or destructive—anything less than accurately reflective of the image of Christ—the world takes a loss at every level."[5] The effect on women and the social fallout of a society where men are behaving poorly is all about us. However, the not-so-obvious problem is internal.

When it comes to understanding masculinity, men *need* women. That's right. Men do need men, and we will discuss this later in the book, but men also need women to help them understand masculinity.

Men benefit from being able to compare and contrast. The subconscious reasoning is, *"If that is what feminine is, then masculine must be this."* In other words, men know they need women in order to better understand their own strength and role. As a general rule, women are more gifted at intuitively understanding their roles while men gather information from all available sources. While there is strength in the men's methodology, there is power in the women's giftedness.

As the women's movement gathered momentum some thirty years ago, there were advances in women's rights that were long overdue. But as is the case with any social revolution, the destination was not always clearly defined. While there are wonderful similarities and some shared characteristics, women were never intended to be exactly like men, nor were men intended to be like women. Gaining equality for women must leave room for celebrating our differences. As James Dobson once said, "Boys and girls should be taught that the sexes are equal in worth but very different from one another."[6]

Women behaving like men in society and the work place hampers the natural abilities of women and confuses men. This approach to social change creates social tension, gender insecurity, confusion, and emotional ineffectiveness. Furthermore, by seeking to diminish the differences between the sexes, the goal of equality is actually derailed.

Let me be quick to point out, this perspective on the role of women does not stipulate they stay at home, avoid the work place, the board rooms, the military service, or professional life. The above paragraphs pertain to a philosophical approach to life, an attitude, and a woman's confidence in her feminine identity. To have the same job as a man, with the same salary, the same benefits, and the same respect does not necessitate a woman sacrifice her femininity and behave like a man. That notion is a disservice done to women by the leaders and philosophers of the feminist movement. The equality sought by the women's movement is an equality based upon respect for the individual versus a contrived equality that undermines masculinity while elevating women through masculine role play.

I worked as a counselor for several years at Kanakuk, a Christian camp just outside Branson, Missouri. One of the games we played was Indian ball—sort of like softball, with a larger, softer ball. A mitt was impractical and unnecessary. Besides, playing bare-handed was part of the game.

During staff week, before the campers arrived, the counselors would assemble in coed teams on the upper ball field to play Indian ball together. The rules of softball applied with these exceptions: Each team supplied their own pitcher and the guys had to switch-hit. In other words, if a man normally batted right-handed, he had to bat left-handed. The goal was to hamper the men when they were batting so the women in the field would enjoy the game. It worked great! Everyone had loads of fun.

But consider this question: Would it be accurate for the women to conclude after a game of Indian ball that they were equal to the men in batting prowess? Certainly not. In fact, just the opposite turned out to be the case. Some of the differences between the sexes were actually accentuated. In Indian ball this made for great fun, but to carry the same logic forward to life ultimately creates problems. Changing roles in an attempt to establish equality eventually creates insecurity and frustration for both men and women. Before long, the women feel patronized and the men unappreciated, neither of which communicates respect, the very thing equality is supposed to be based upon.

A woman is never in an inferior place as long as she is in the place God intended for her. The same may be said for a man. For all of its worthwhile advances, the women's movement did both women and men a disservice by blurring the distinction of roles between them.

Once gender roles are blurred, these questions go begging for an answer: Who are women? What is a man? What does each do? How are they to treat one another? These sorts of questions are tough for men and women to answer, but they are especially difficult for men who are not well equipped to evaluate these kinds of issues.

For a woman to be tough as nails during a business meeting, then slip into her feminine persona and expect the man to treat her with gentle understanding, leaves a man confused and off balance. He subconsciously wonders, *"If women are not consistent with their expectations, and their behavior is fickle, and their persona vacillating, how am I supposed to know who they are, what femininity is, and how they expect to be treated?"* If not impossible to answer, at the very least this question requires intuitive analysis, and for most men, that is simply not possible. In fact, most guys will be doing well just to draw the question from their subconscious.

As long as women doubt their feminine identity, men will feel insecure meeting women's needs and contrasting themselves against the feminine mystique. If women are busy trying to act like men in order to gain equality with them, they rob themselves and men of femininity.

It isn't that men are stupid or inept, but that they are not equipped and gifted to think through issues of this sort. On the one hand, men are fairly basic. If convinced they are on the right road, they move forward regardless of what may get in their way. On the other hand, if they feel uncertain, doubt sets in, insecurity begins to haunt them, and confidence eludes them. In this event, men either bluff their way down the road representing their best guess, or they act out their frustration. When it comes to internal matters, many men struggle to discern the issues they are warring against.

Will We Make It?

And what of the women? How are they doing in their quest for equality? How is their goal of social change progressing? In the January 11, 1992, edition of the *Washington Post,* Sally Quinn wrote that women feel betrayed by the proponents of the women's movement:

> They feel betrayed and lied to because trying to live a polit-
> ically correct personal life doesn't always work, as Steinem,
> Fonda, Streisand, Kelly and others have demonstrated. If
> the feminists could say they were wrong about women
> needing men or men needing women, what were they right
> about? If they were living one life and espousing another,
> wasn't that corrupt?[7]

Jane Fonda married Ted Turner and announced she was giving up acting now that she was married. "Ted is not a man that you leave to go on location," she said. "He needs you there all the time."[8] Gloria Steinem wrote in her autobiography that much of her feminist ideals were designed to get even with a man who treated her badly.[9] Barbra Streisand, who just recently married again, said, "Even though my feminist side says people should be independent and not need to be taken care of by an-other person, it doesn't always necessarily work that way. There is the human factor, you know."[10]

Quinn writes later in her article, "Feminist leaders were pub-licly telling mothers of three it was great to leave their husbands and be independent—and then secretly dressing up in Fred-erick's of Hollywood for their guys."[11]

Having been robbed by the leaders of the feminist move-ment, women are like a flock of geese trying to get organized after taking off from the lake to fly home. They are airborne, but unsure of their leaders and direction.

Will they make it? Will they rediscover their feminine iden-tity? Most likely, yes. After all, one of the great differences between women and men is that women possess an intuitive ability to understand themselves and their needs. It is natural for them to rally together and support each other. They talk and share their feelings. They are less competitive and more accommodating. They will correct course and find their way. In fact, throughout society the first signs of this are already occurring.

And the men? They are out in the woods painting themselves with war paint, blowing horns, sitting around fires smoking pipes, attending men's groups, working out, trying to be more sensitive and less competitive, and trying to adopt those things society says will make them less masculine. In all of these pursuits men are looking for true masculinity because in the night someone robbed them of their true persona.

The notion of "who men are" has been clouded by social disdain and ridicule. In church pews, factories, and farms, men retreat into the darkness of their own mysterious needs wondering who they are and how to be masculine. In his best-selling book, *Men Are From Mars, Women Are From Venus,* John Gray calls this "living in the masculine cave."[12] Every man has a cave he withdraws to in an effort to regain control. The cave may be work, a hobby, church, athletics, stoicism, booze, drugs, silence, depression, violence, sexual deviation, toughness, or any other alternative to true masculine self-awareness.

Dealing with identity problems is not a masculine forté. Women are much better suited to this sort of thing. Even if a man senses the problem, it is far too personal—and most likely too confusing—to even consider talking about with the woman in his life. Critically evaluating his masculine identity is too frightening—it's like sitting at the poker table with a weak hand and tipping your cards to your opponent. A husband looks across the dining room table at his wife, who he is supposed to be strong for, the person he is supposed to protect and provide for, the person from whom he needs respect and veneration as a strong man, and he decides not to tip his hand and discuss his identity problems. Instead, he decides to hide out. The cave is a better option.

The problem is that the masculine cave is not a place of enlightenment. It is not a bastion from which to wage a courageous war, nor is it the high ground from which to engage the enemy. A cave is not a castle. A cave is a place of darkness, more suited to bats and spiders, to crawling on your belly through the dank, wet, cold. A cave is a place for following a prescribed route, or holding onto a rope like they do in kindergarten, not for standing upright and searching the horizon for life's visions.

Men with Hollow Chests

"Even the most visible winners among men in American life are doubting themselves" author Gail Sheehy wrote in *Parade* magazine. "I would definitely say we are dispirited," CBS television correspondent Bill Geist told *The New York Times*. "We've lost track of whether we're supposed to be acting more manly or more sensitive...It might be that men are winding down and becoming unnecessary."[13]

I can see you now, flipping furiously toward the endnotes, muttering, "What kind of moron would say that? Stupid stuff! I can't believe the drivel they write now days. What does he mean, 'unnecessary'? I take out the trash, mow the grass, know the guy who works on the car, pay for dinner when the family goes out. Where would the kids be if I hadn't been around when Louise and I got married? Unnecessary my eye! They *wouldn't be* if it weren't for me!"

But the fact remains, western man is struggling mightily to regain a sense of who he is and what manhood is all about. Robert Bly said in his best-selling book, *Iron John*, "The activity men were once loved for is not required [any longer]."[14] In years past, men were the protectors and providers for women and children in tangible, measurable ways. Each day they banded together and went out to prevail against a vast, unconquered, and dangerous land. Everyone knew if the men did their job, all would be able to sleep safely and have their basic needs supplied. But very few men in the western world are asked to live their lives by such noble and tangible means. Today the dangerous places are board rooms, factories, and sales calls.

Several years ago I had the privilege of speaking at a Christian university in Hawaii. That first opportunity turned into a regular occurrence, and for three or four years I traveled to the islands once or twice a year to teach. (It was tough duty, but somebody had to do it.) I worked hard and played hard as well. I also met many wonderful people who introduced me to swimming with dolphins, chasing flounders, climbing waterfalls, and dodging wild boars. They showed me sides of Hawaii and its culture not everyone who visits gets to see. While my ministry, friends, and experiences are irreplaceable, I'm here to report all is not well in paradise.

As Bly would say, the activity Hawaiian men were once loved for is not required any longer. Instead of leaving each morning to go down to the sea to fish, or into the jungles to hunt, they go to the hotel to dress up in traditional garb and reenact the reign of King Kamehameha for visitors to the islands. Many hang out at the beach and wait for the surf to come up, or simply cruise town. Instead of being respected as protectors and providers, they are tourist attractions.

Hawaiian men are foundering over the loss of their masculine identity and trying to regain their bearings by retracing their ancestral worship of Pali, the volcano goddess. Meanwhile, the Japanese and Asian cultures are moving into the islands as entrepreneurs and professional types. The laid-back culture of the Hawaiians has been bowled over by the aggressive work ethic and achievement pressure of the Asians.

The results? Hawaiian men feel their identity disintegrating under aggressive social change. There is a rise in child abuse, spousal abuse, drugs, crime, and alcoholism. My hosts reported all of these social ills are higher among the Hawaiian culture than the other cultures on the island. But our Polynesian brothers are not the only example. Much the same story is true among the various tribes of the Native Americans. Let's face it, there isn't much call for Indian braves to straddle a war pony and go galloping across the plains on a buffalo hunt so that women and children will be fed and clothed. Once again, it is as though the role Native American men filled is no longer needed, and the social fallout is not much different from the symptoms of lost identity evident among Hawaiian men.

Evaluate the tragedy played out day after day in the inner cities of America due to the loss of strong, masculine leadership. The fact that 70% of African-American children nationwide are born to unwed mothers is a graphic indicator that African-American men are missing the point when it comes to what masculinity is all about.[15] You do not have to be a sociologist or psychological guru to observe that the crumbling of the masculine persona is no longer limited to islands in the Pacific, reservations in the Midwest, or the asphalt jungles of America's inner cities. Loss of identity, confused roles, absent role models, detached relationships, deteriorating moral standards, isolated men, and the abortion of ethics are the telltale signs of a world where the corner posts—men, regardless of race, religious background, or home turf—are weak and wobbling.

As men look around them to regain their bearings, as the young men look to the older men to understand masculinity and determine what comprises manhood, they see men with hollow chests and shamed faces. Their hearts and souls have been seared by doubts and insecurities. Instead of a clear vision of manhood, men see ambiguity, confusion, hostility, and frustration in their counterparts.

Men who have lost their way and become confused about the source of true strength offer little to those who are looking to them for guidance. And they are themselves susceptible to desperate measures in an effort to regain a sense of purpose and respect that feeds their souls. Try as they will, the confidence of masculinity eludes them, they are consumed with emasculation, and the social ills propagate as the corner posts wiggle and tilt.

THE PREDATOR

3

Each summer my folks put me on a Greyhound bus bound for Poteau, Oklahoma, a small town pressed up against the Arkansas state line and nestled beside the highest hill in the world, Cavanaugh, which we called "Granddaddy's Mountain." According to Granddad, this was the mountain the bear went over to see what he could see.

Even though he was only 5'9" and 145 pounds, Granddad Hoyle was almost larger than life. A week at his house passed like a New York minute. There were a few special events with each visit, like going to Fort Smith to eat at the cafeteria, but mainly the week was filled with Granddad's routine. Each morning we climbed into his old Chevy truck, which he would invariably bump start as he coasted down the driveway toward the road. I guess that was easier than using the starter, which was a big, round button on the floorboard next to the accelerator. His truck was nothing short of cool as far as I was concerned.

First stop was the courthouse, where Granddad, who was justice of the peace, held court. Once in a while the deputies would bring some guy downstairs from the holding cell, sporting a cocky attitude over what landed him in the Le Flore County jail. This was a mistake (following whatever his mistake was the night before). Just like the Lone Ranger's mask, you didn't mess with Judge Hoyle. Granddad was always fair and kind, but when crossed, his ice-blue eyes sent an unmistakable message to the offender: "You just made a serious error in judgment." When Judge Hoyle was holding court, the courthouse *and* the prisoner paid attention. And as you would imagine, being Marcus Hoyle's grandson, I was always greeted with great respect.

Next we were off to the post office to check the box, then down the street to say hello to F.L. Holton, and finally by the insurance agency to see my Aunt Betty and Uncle Bill. By late morning we were headed back up the hill to Granddad's house at the base of the mountain.

The rest of the day was spent gathering vegetables from the garden, fishing in the pond, playing mumblety-peg, gathering eggs from the hen house, or exploring the farm with Sport, Granddad's red dog. After dinner, if we didn't drop by to visit Granddad's brother, Uncle Vassar, we would sit in the side yard until time for the news. That's when Granddad's stories began to flow.

With the glow of his pipe visible against his silhouette, Granddad would recount his tales as the smell of "Prince Albert" floated into the evening. The first stories were the true stories, and when pressed for more, he would ease into the figments of his imagination and carry me along for the ride.

He finally caught the fox raiding his hen house. He grabbed a rattlesnake by the tail as it crawled under the house and popped its head off by cracking it like a whip. He drove in one evening to find a deer standing in his carport. He and Sport treed a mother coon in the oak tree next to the front porch. His stories were usually punctuated by the calls of bob whites and whip-poorwills, which he paused to listen to and emulate. Each story was matter-of-fact and drawn out by Granddad's low drawl. Nothing dramatic, just another day around the house on the hill.

Where the stories digressed from truth to fiction was not always apparent, but I was fairly certain when he suddenly stopped to listen to the catamount (a.k.a. the mountain lion, puma, and cougar) wailing in the distance, he was pulling my leg. He never said much about coyotes, and looking back on it now, for good reason: To do so would have spoiled the wailing catamount story he was about to embark upon.

While the stories of mountain predators lurking in the shadows, weaving surreptitiously closer to the side yard, were mythologies created in Granddad's vivid imagination, they were compelling and energizing and fueled my imagination while occupying untold hours. And then, as if on cue, Granddad would knock his pipe out on the arm of his lawn chair, signaling it was time to go inside for cornbread and milk, the news, and bed. "Well, boy, we have a big day tomorrow."

The Enemy

The Bible says that Satan prowls about like a roaring lion looking for someone to devour (1 Peter 5:8). While Satan is not a mythological character, I often imagine his practice of prowling must look a lot like the images painted by Granddad when he talked about the catamount wailing over the mountain.

Like any predator, Satan knows devouring prey is essential to his way of life, and in his case, he is intent on devouring the hearts of men. The devil knows if men fail in their responsibilities, the kingdom of God becomes vulnerable to his accusations. A spiritual battle rages for the hearts and lives of men who are called to demonstrate the relationship God wants to have with all people.

Men know their story is about real life, seven days a week. That's why this book is not about religious activity, or adding things to your life that give the illusion of making progress when in fact you are not. At a basic level, a man's story is actually a classic tale pitting good against evil. Our story is about a Heavenly

Father who loves us faithfully, and His determined, vindictive enemy whose plan is to undermine God by deceiving us.

We are the means to the enemy's agenda. Pawns in his chess game. The method to his madness. The only reason Satan targets us is to get at God. If the enemy can entice us to walk after the flesh, and in so doing discredit our Heavenly Father's sufficiency in our lives, then he has grounds to accuse God of being something less than He claims. Satan's logic is profoundly simple: Attack God's worthiness to be God by tempting men to live independently of Him. If we do not submit our lives to God we facilitate the enemy's case, asserting God's unworthiness to anyone who will listen. If Satan were to articulate his rationale, he might say, "The reason men do not submit to God is because God is not worthy of their allegiance." And then the real issue can surface: "I think someone else should sit on the throne of God...and who better than me, the one who exposed God's unworthiness."

Satan's goal is the same today as it has been since he instigated rebellion in heaven eons ago: He wants to be God and sit in God's chair. The most direct route to realizing his goal is through the allegiance of men.

It is inconsequential to Satan how his goals are achieved. He will be equally satisfied if a man chooses to exhibit independence toward God in the way he teaches his Sunday School class or if he lives independently by lying in the gutter drunk all night. Independence is the bottom line for the devil and it is irrelevant to him how independence is manifested. If a man decides to live independent of God, he plays into the devil's hand and gives him a platform from which to accuse God.

As you can see, we are engaged in a great battle between good and evil. Demonstrating through our daily lives what God had in mind when He thought of making a man in the first place is a bigger picture than getting up, going to work to earn a living, and coming home, day in and day out. In a very real sense, a man is a warrior, fighting for a great cause: *God's worthiness.*

The Predator of Isolation

As if wondering about the viability of manhood were not enough of a burden to haul around, the enemy of God and man perpetrates a uniquely masculine attack: isolation. We have tried to adapt, accept, and accommodate masculine loneliness by glamorizing it in the movies and portraying men as independent and self-sufficient. But the fact is, men need men. For all the competition and aggressiveness men exhibit toward each other, one of the deep needs in a man's life is masculine companionship.

Gordon MacDonald puts it this way: "We were built for intimacy, this linkage of souls, but most of us men rarely experience it. And its scarcity breeds *loneliness* (I don't really know anyone) and fuels *remoteness* (no one really knows me)."[16]

Isolation is an awkward problem. Most of us agree we need other men in our lives, but knowing what to do with him when God brings one along is another matter. Friendship of this type is a modeled and learned behavior. If we haven't seen it enacted, creating it for ourselves is a formidable challenge, producing awkward emotions that can be avoided if isolation is maintained.

If you think about the men discussed in the Bible, no matter how eccentric they were, whether in the Old Testament or the New, young or old, the men of God's Word were rarely alone. You can't really think of Moses without thinking of Aaron as well. And the same could be said for Elijah and Elisha, David and Jonathan, Paul and Barnabas, Paul and Silas, and of course, Jesus along with Peter, James, and John. If these men placed a premium on having other men in their lives, it seems apparent there is wisdom here we would be wise to consider.

It used to be that men worked together, fought together, lived together, raised their crops together, and depended upon each other. However, as the industrial revolution began to gather momentum and western culture moved away from its agrarian roots, profound changes occurred in society. Instead of living together as an extended family on the farm, individual families moved to urban areas. Men began working for someone else rather than working together within an extended family or side-by-side with their neighbor. While they still worked shoulder-to-shoulder, the man next to him was not assisting, he was competing. The natural aggressiveness and competition of men was turned away from the environment and toward each other in order to fuel production. Instead of a comrade-in-arms, the man next to him was competing for his job. He was after his chair, his idea, his credit. For most men, the world of work does not create dependence upon others but competition, and in many cases distrust and suspicion. No longer are men compelled to work together for the common good. They realize they must look out for themselves. Independence becomes a way of life.

Never rest—drive on. Never trust another—maintain control. Never depend on someone else—you are an island. Never show weakness—you are responsible for yourself and your career. Emerson declared in his famous work, "Self-Reliance," "Trust thyself: every heart vibrates to that iron string."[17] Never mind that iron strings have no resonance. There is only the sound of a dull plunk in a man's heart.

In his poem, "Invictus," William Ernest Henley verbalizes the credo adopted by many men.

> Out of the night that covers me,
>   Black as the Pit from pole to pole,
> I thank whatever gods may be
>   For my unconquerable soul.
>
> In the fell clutch of circumstance
>   I have not winced nor cried aloud.
> Under the bludgeonings of chance
>   My head is bloody, but unbowed.
>
> Beyond this place of wrath and tears
>   Looms but the horror of the shade,
> And yet the menace of the years
>   Finds, and shall find me, unafraid.

It matters not how straight the gate,
  How charged with punishments the scroll,
I am the master of my fate;
  I am the captain of my soul.[18]

Fundamentally, this attitude of independence goes against the nature and need of masculinity. Reading the lines of "Invictus," feeling the strength of the words, and identifying with the poetic portrait of conquest painted in word-pictures by Mr. Henley appeals to independence, control, and self-reliance. But advocating this independent philosophy to men is certainly not in keeping with how men function best, and is therefore neither as effective or efficient as the Creator originally conceived.

God's Plan for Men

In many corporations the trend is to organize teams and assign mentors. Why? Because someone in management recognizes the need for closeness, personal training, and the influence of older men on younger men. They realize that men working in union, depending upon each other, benefiting from the years of experience an older man has acquired, is a profitable thing. Men are more productive and more resilient when their environment is filled with trust and interdependence. Together men ward off isolation. Together they are more effective than if they are separated from the pack.

Men were created by God to be together, to understand their strength comes not from autonomy and independence but from *dependence*. A man knows that deep within his genetic composition is a code driving him to give his life for a cause, to protect, provide, create stability, serve, be loyal, and if necessary, lay down his life for his beliefs. But in each of these quests, no man functions best alone. And if called upon to give his life, no man wants to die alone.

Placing this in the context of a man's commitment to his family, Stu Weber says,

> We're to be willing to die for our wives and our children
> instantly, and many of us are ready to do just that. But
> within the willingness to die for family and home, some-
> thing inside us longs for someone to die *with*...someone to
> die *beside*...someone to lock step with. Another man with a
> heart like our own.[19]

If this is God's plan for men, is it any surprise the enemy of
God—the predator—assaults with resolve a man's understanding of how his Heavenly Father created him? After all, if the devil
can deceive a man, distract a man, separate him, and quarantine
him from other men, the chances of isolation haunting his soul
and creating masculine doubt are enhanced.

Throughout all of time and mythology men have been called
upon to war against their enemies—a noble calling indeed. But
risking life and limb to dispose of an enemy while being isolated
challenges even the strongest man among us to lose his focus and
doubt his strength. This gives rise to a pervasive frustration that
eventually boils into masculine hostility.

Recognizing the odds against which men are fighting is not
the challenge. Knowing what to do about it is.

The Predator of Religion

I'm for the church and I'm for the Bible, but this fellow that
many churches put forth as a godly man is a ruse, a contrivance,
an imposter, a manipulation to moderate masculinity to fit a religious mold that is neither biblical nor Christian. The man created
by religion is a sham and does not resemble the prototype on
God's mind when He designed man in the first place.

When masculinity is spoken of in an honorable way, there is a
deep resonance in every man's heart. But many men have never
felt this resonance because it is synonymous with a masculine passion not always welcome in religious circles. As our feminized
society has busied itself tempering the masculine passion, many
sectors of religion have followed suit. Masculine temperance is

spoken and implied, taught and suggested, sanctioned and banned, modeled and enforced by guilt because traditional masculinity doesn't fit the contrived stereotype of what a godly man is.

The godly man as defined by religion is meek and mild, even tempered, self-effacing, always smiling, always pleasant, reticent, measured, and deferring. Often the Christian man who demonstrates passivity and acquiescence is held up as an example of a true, godly man. But passivity is not godliness, it is flesh—a pattern generated through self-effort to gain acceptance. Fleshly patterns are sin. Every single time. They are never godly characteristics.

When men see passivity esteemed as a godly characteristic, godliness loses its appeal and intrinsic meaning. Deep in his heart, every man knows masculinity has something to do with strength. In the recesses of his soul, a man senses there is a resonant chord waiting to fill his chest cavity with the harmony of true masculinity. The dispassion of religion is incapable of striking this powerful chord within the heart of a man.

Perhaps one of the most insidious attacks the predator makes against Christian men is the religious diatribe against emotion. It is true, our culture systematically indoctrinates men with instructions about which emotions are "proper" and which ones are "improper." Religion joins the ranks of culture and uses misinterpreted Scripture verses as a hammer to beat men into emotionlessness in the name of godliness. Anger is wrong. Intensity is wrong. Passion is wrong. Exuberance is wrong. Effervescent joy is wrong. Despondency is wrong. Discouragement is wrong. Celebration is wrong. Satisfaction is wrong. Confidence is wrong. Pride is wrong. Assertiveness is wrong.

So men clam up. The religious smile is pasted on, and with typical masculine determination, a decision is made to emulate the imposters while at church. But in so doing, true masculinity is lost.

Have you noticed that it is not OK to have problems and struggles at church? In most religious circles if a man musters enough gumption to say he is struggling with some issue—as long as it is not something really sinful like pornography, lust, cursing, anger, or drinking too much—the brethren will agree to pray for him. But the message remains clear: To be a godly man you have to have your act together, and until you do, godliness is elusive.

Besides, every man who has been around religion for a while knows the Bible says Christ is all you need, and, "you can do all things through Christ who strengthens you."[20] While being hard-pressed to make sense of these verses Monday through Saturday, any man with even a little savvy can see it is wrong to admit he struggles, lest he discredit the sufficiency of Christ. And if a godly man can do "all things" through Christ who strengthens him—this evidently includes leaping tall buildings and stopping speeding freight trains—then asking for help, expressing need, acknowledging a weakness, or admitting a struggle is an affront to Christ's ability. The conclusion and implication is obvious: Whatever you do, don't say anything. And by all means, don't be honest about your struggles. Get with the program or go somewhere else.

The godly man contrived by religion lives in a black and white world. After all, he's been taught the Bible has all the answers. That means he has no need of listening, empathizing, caring, or talking. Besides, these things have a way of becoming gray, and there is always the danger of tainting a well-crafted, religious reputation with life's gray areas. It only stands to reason that it is inappropriate to ask questions since the Bible has all the answers and religion has already outlined them. Tough issues like divorce, abuse, adultery, and homosexuality are handled via impersonal means like church bylaws, flying under the flag of some scriptural passage that may or may not be relevant. The religious man's relationships tend to be shallow, safe, and controlled because real relationships tend to be grayish in color, not black and white, and religion is explicit: Gray is not an appropriate color for a godly man.

Thus the ruse is foisted on other men and a religion-contrived imposter carries the banner of "godly man" in many of our churches. The true nature of masculinity is never broached. In fact, it is virtually unknown and often unwelcome.

So men occupy their folding chair in Sunday School, sit in their pew during worship, serve dutifully on church committees, and do not connect with each other any more deeply than the contrived religious persona of masculinity will allow. They do not share their hurts, ask questions of each other, reveal their heart, acknowledge their struggles, voice their wonder, pray with passion, mention the deep insights God is revealing to them, or resonate with masculinity.

Laboring under this contrivance of what a godly man is and does, Christian men struggle to make their faith personal and relevant. God is missed and men are left with a legalistic system that is an irrelevant, self-serving façade. While some men put up a good front, play the religious game, and try to fool others, in their hearts they know the chord being struck has no resonance. In fact, it has no more melodious reverberation than the iron string of independence.

And with this, men are haunted by questions they cannot voice because the religious system will not allow it. The feeling is terrifying because it feels irrelevant. It is as though the faith I seek as a man is of no value and is powerless to counter the assault launched against me daily. If a godly man is nothing more than religion portrays him to be, then God must be no more than the man created in His image and lifted up by religion. Let's face it: Every man knows that if God is like me, then He is too small to deal with what I face as a man.

I am making a clear distinction between religion and Christianity. The two are not synonymous. Religion is nothing more than man's search for God, and this has nothing whatsoever to do with Christianity. The Christian faith is about the God of the universe, supreme above all creation, holy, high and lifted up. It is about the God who prefers to be called "Father" and who chose to leave His throne in heaven to chase across the universe in search of a relationship with man. For men, Christianity is about relationship, man to man. Jesus Christ, God-become-man, pursues us to bond with us and demonstrate His life through us seven days a week. He is the One who created us and He is the one most gifted at making the resonating chord of masculinity echo in our chests. The religious impersonator neither lives passionately nor resonates true manhood.

A Man's Destiny

Satan, the predator of man, roams the face of the earth looking for unsuspecting men to devour. Many men are ashamed of their masculinity. Many more are confused. Lots of others are stalked by doubt, frustration, and hostility. If we take time to listen, the masculine passion is not beating in our hearts and the resonance of the masculine chord is deadened. Hollywood's portraits are not helping us understand manhood. The vocal minority is not echoing our sentiment. Religious purveyors manipulate us to advance their own agenda, not tell us about true godliness, the kind indicative of manhood.

In the pressure of the hunt, many men make an executive decision and declare themselves "men" simply because they are pragmatists. They need to get on with life, get on with raising their children, get on with climbing the professional ladder, and get on with establishing their desired lifestyle. They decide to bestow the declaration of manhood on themselves in an effort to quit worrying about not receiving it, and in so doing they pronounce to themselves that the masculine insecurity they feel is normal.

The masculine face may be obscured and those sages screaming that I am the master of my own fate, the author of my own destiny, the principle proponent of my own independence may sound reasonable. I may have been robbed of my bearings, and religion may be perpetrating a great deception regarding true masculinity, but it is against such odds a strong man thrives. It is for times such as these I was created. It is my destiny to war against evil and fight for the good. It is in the face of these odds I discover the true strength of masculinity and begin to feel the deep resonance of real manhood.

A man is created for challenges. He is equipped to overcome, to run the gauntlet, to stand firm as a well-anchored corner post. Men are the benchmark in life, society, and family. It is part of the masculine responsibility to demonstrate strength and stability, to protect and provide for those within their sphere of influence. This is the hallmark of manhood.

And what is the source of this great strength? When ordinary men depend upon the sufficiency of Christ, extraordinary things occur. As is the case in any classic tale of good and evil, right and wrong, there must be a hero. That's you! No, you are not Superman, and I am not headed for the conclusion that because Philippians 4:13 says you "can do all things through Christ" that you have the potential to become super human.

The encouraging word is that God is doing His work in the hearts and lives of the men He fought and died to reclaim. Even though the enemy of God is busy trying to discredit His efforts, cloud His overtures, and question the motives of His heart for the lives of men. God intends to communicate His message, man to man. He will not waver in His commitment. Men *are* necessary. God designed us to walk with Him and called us to represent Him on earth. It is His determination to stand by us, make us strong, and bless us as men created in His image.

WHAT WENT WRONG?

4

Eve handed her husband his lunch and kissed him good-bye as he left for work, promising to stop by mid-afternoon to see how his project was progressing. She was proud of him. He managed God's garden—Eden—and had direct responsibility for naming the creation of God's imaginative genius, a testimony to the creative intellect of her man. Besides his intelligence, she was totally taken with his killer good looks and one-of-a-kind swagger. No doubt about it: Adam was his Father's son.

Well, enough of this pining away watching Adam traipse off to the office, Eve had things to do herself if she was going to make it in time for his afternoon break. As far as she was concerned, life was nothing short of a joy. In fact, had she anything else to judge it against, Eve would have said it was perfect. It was Eden, and she and Adam were innocent.

About three o'clock, Eve freshened her face and ran her fingers through her rich hair. She batted her eyelashes a few times and pinched her cheeks. A circuitous walk through the garden would relax her and time her arrival just right for her rendezvous with Adam.

"Well, hell-o-o there. You are walking with a spring in your step today, Ms. Eve. Is it the usual?"

"Yes. I'm joining Adam for an afternoon break. It's one of our traditions. Excuse me, but I don't know that I have had the pleasure of making your acquaintance."

"Oh, pardon me please. My name is Lu. Actually, that is not my full name, but that is neither here nor there because I prefer to go by Lucky. You've got to admit it has a ring to it: Lucky Lu.

"But say, I've been wondering about a rumor going around and you are just the person who can answer my question. Is it true God said you and Adam could not eat fruit from any of the trees in this lovely garden?"

"Oh my, no! That would be completely unreasonable. Who in the world would start such a vile rumor, accusing Him of such a thoughtless standard? What He said was we may eat fruit from any tree in the garden except the tree growing in the center of Eden. As a matter of fact, we are not even to touch that tree."

"And why in the world would He not want you to touch that tree or eat its fruit? What could possibly be wrong with so lush a tree as that one?"

Answering as if surprised that Lu didn't know the answer himself, Eve blurted out, "We will die!"

Lu rolled his eyes and chuckled. "The old don't-eat-from-this-tree-or-you'll-die myth? It is a prevarication, an equivocation, a fabrication, a misrepresentation. My soul, girl, don't look so dumbfounded! It is a fib, a whopper, a white lie. He is concocting this death routine so that you will remain in the dark. Why, it's common knowledge that if you eat the fruit from the center-of-the-garden tree your eyes will be opened and you will be like God Himself. Now, last time I checked, that would be a good thing. The very nuances differentiating right from wrong will be opened wide for you to see. Another good thing. Listen, this is not a choice of life and death as you've been told, but one of enlightenment versus stupidity, knowledge versus ignorance.

I mean, look for yourself, lady. That tree has the best fruit in the garden hanging from its branches!"

And with that persuasion, Eve made a critical decision, choosing to believe Lu rather than God (whom she was having some doubts about anyway after talking with Lu). It did seem a bit arrogant to keep such a wonderful tree all to yourself by profligating a self-serving sham. Besides, Eve was half way through her second piece of fruit and wasn't dead yet. In fact, she was feeling just fine.

Anxious to share her enlightening conversation and life-altering discovery with Adam, Eve bid Lu good-bye, and having spent longer than she had intended talking with him, she set off on a direct course for where Adam was busy naming animals, carrying along another sample of the lush, center-tree fruit to share with her man.

"Hey, Babe!" Adam heard her coming before he saw her. She was a breath-taking beauty and the pride of his life. There wasn't anything he would not do for her.

"Adam! Look what I've got. You will not believe it! I met the most wonderful creature—really pretty too—who straightened me out about that tree in the center of the garden. You know the one—the one we are not supposed to eat from because we might die? Well, look at me! I've eaten two pieces of its fruit already—Lucky Lu said it would be OK—and I haven't died. In fact, Lu said I wouldn't be in the dark anymore."

"Who is Lucky Lu, and you've eaten how many pieces of fruit?"

"Two. And he's the neatest person. A real straight-shooter. Cuts right through all of the divine mumbo-jumbo and puts the conversation in terms I can understand. Eat this and let me tell you about our talk."

"Tell you what, Sweetheart. Why don't you hang onto that and let's go sit down and talk this over."

Adam and Eve talked for a couple of hours about miscellaneous topics, returning with some regularity to Eve's decision to eat the fruit from the forbidden tree. With each offer of the fruit from Eve, Adam thanked her and declined.

As was His custom, God came walking through the garden in the cool of the evening. Even though He knew where Adam and Eve were, He still liked to call for them. The sound of their names escaping His lips made His fatherly heart proud. The universe was His and all it contained, but the highlight of His day was hanging out with Adam and Eve in Eden.

"Adam. Eve. Adam. Eve."

Sitting on a rock not far from Adam's "office," Adam and Eve were still engaged in their conversation when the Father's voice made its way to their ears. Adam jumped to his feet, anxious to see God. Eve bailed over their sitting rock backward and headed for tall timber. Confused, but undeterred, Adam called out to God, "Over here, by the sitting rock."

Their reunion was grand, as always, and God's first question was predictable: "Where's Eve?"

Adam wasn't much help other than pointing in the general direction he'd last seen Eve running and offering a shrug. But God didn't really need any help to find her. They walked a short way and stopped a respectable distance from where Eve had hidden herself in a thicket.

His voice was compassionate, but strong and forceful. It was evident He meant business. "Eve, have you eaten from the tree I warned you not to eat from?"

God got neither a yes or a no, only the run-around. "Lu, the serpent, deceived me and I ate the fruit."

Knowing he would be called anyway to account for himself, the serpent presented himself close by, received God's scathing curse, and slithered in the opposite direction of Eve's vengeful eyes.

And then God addressed Eve: "I am a person of my word and the consequence of failing to follow my command regarding the center-of-the-garden tree was clear right from the start. Eve, I hate to do it, but the choice was yours. We had a wonderful thing going and many great times I will treasure, walking through the garden, talking during the cool of the evening. But Eve, you must bear responsibility for your transgression. My pronouncement of death is as follows...."

But as God was taking in a deep breath to make the dreaded declaration, Adam touched his Father's arm forcefully enough to gain eye contact with his Maker. Adam stood up straight and set his jaw, squared his shoulders, and spoke deliberately. "Father, I will readily submit to Your will in this situation, but if it would be suitable to You, I would like to take Eve's place. Please Father, let me die in her stead so she may live and walk with You in the garden during the cool of the evening. I offer myself as her redemption."

Or at least that's the way I think it should have gone. And if you are like me, this feels more like the way the story should have ended instead of with the curses and expulsion from Eden. Somewhere in chapters two and three of Genesis, Adam had an opportunity to become a vehicle of redemption for his wife, to protect her and provide for her, to act as a warrior by laying down his life so she could live. Instead he ate the fruit along with her, acted without honor, caved in when his wife was at her greatest point of need, and so came to an ignominious end that passed along to men the shame of his failure.[21]

It is this failure of our forefather that haunts the souls of men. This shame is buried deep in the silt of the masculine psyche. It is an emasculating wound. The scandal of what Adam could have done—was created and designed to do—is the culpable claw reaching up to drag our heart and soul into a morass of confusion and dull the resonance of masculinity. Jack Hayford writes,

> It seems that somehow all sons of the first Adam sense that
> our earthly forefather has bequeathed a failure to us. It
> seems that as men we somehow have had a scar burned into
> our collective masculine psyche; a sense of disability ful-
> filling our spiritual role; a subtle inner voice which shouts,
> "Your father failed as a man and so will you! He missed
> becoming an instrument of redemption, and neither will
> you ever be able to become an instrument in God's hands."[22]

Adam lost his footing as a secure, stable corner post. How many anxious and anticipatory moments have there been waiting for someone to stabilize the corner post of manhood? As the Old Testament writer Job was answering his accusers and asserting his integrity, he said, "Have I covered my transgressions like Adam by hiding my iniquity in my bosom?" Deep in the heart of men there is a failure that haunts our masculine confidence. There is the voice of fear saying, "The honor of manhood is too far gone. No matter how determined I am, I will never overcome the failure of Adam and the shame he passed to his descendents."

Unless someone resets the corner post, the honor of mas-culinity will remain elusive and men will forever struggle to equate the esteem of a warrior with manhood and honor with masculinity.

The Last Adam

Several thousand years after Adam's failure in the garden, the Bible recounts a sequel to the story. The hero is called "the last Adam," and like the first Adam, He had a bride who willfully declared her independence from God's will. As a result He made a divine pronouncement of death against her. The decision was not easy, but in a garden outside Jerusalem—far from the perfec-tion of Eden—the last Adam wrestled and fought and sweat great drops of blood anguishing over whether to offer Himself as a vehicle of redemption on behalf of His doomed bride. The deci-sion He made changed the course of history, altered the state of the universe, gained life for His terminal bride, and made a rela-tionship with God viable. By offering Himself as an instrument of redemption, His bride could once again walk and talk with God in the cool of the evening.

"The first man, Adam, became a living soul. The last Adam became a life-giving spirit," Paul declares in 1 Corinthians 15:45. Whereas the first Adam created a burden of shame, Jesus Christ—the last Adam—demonstrated the confidence of courage and reestablished the honor of masculinity. In another of his books, Paul appeals to men by detailing the redemptive lifestyle Jesus Christ demonstrated for the love of His life:

> Husbands, love your wives, just as Christ also loved the church and gave Himself up for her; that He might sanctify her, having cleansed her by the washing of water with the word, that He might present to Himself the church in all her glory, having no spot or wrinkle or any such thing; but that she should be holy and blameless. So husbands ought also to love their wives as their own bodies. He who loves his own wife loves himself; for no one ever hated his own flesh, but nourishes and cherishes it, just as Christ also does the church, because we are members of His body. For this cause a man shall leave his father and mother, and shall cleave to his wife; and the two shall become one flesh. This mystery is great; but I am speaking with reference to Christ and the church.[23]

It is Jesus Christ who indwells us. It is the Spirit of God who empowers us. It is the last Adam who acts as the rock and cement at the base of the corner post. Due to the accomplish-ments of the last Adam, we can become instruments of redemp-tion, reclaim our lost courage, make our hearts transparent and vulnerable, and recapture the honor of manhood.

> Jesus is determined to expand the borders of His kingdom,
> Sir. And He's calling you and me—today—just as He did His
> disciples long ago! The hell-burnt ruins of Adam I—the
> fallen man—smolder around us. But Adam II has come to
> restore all things to the original created order. Let's all—each
> one of us—be among those men who hear what the Holy
> Spirit is saying to the Church, and who respond in step with
> His present redemptive works![24]

A man is designed by God to move forward, and if necessary, to do so in spite of pain, difficulty, and inconvenience. This does not mean men are supposed to live in denial about the burdens they carry and the struggles that snare them. Nor does it offer men an excuse to sling their emotional baggage at anyone close enough to be smacked by their hostility. What it does mean is no matter what complications you encountered on your journey from boyhood toward manhood, you must make a determination to trust Christ to bless you as a man and build into you a life that demonstrates masculine strength.

As a believer, Jesus Christ lives in you because He wants to live His life through you and recast you in the image of your Heavenly Father. Through His restorative process, Christ intends to rebuild your sagging male courage and resurrect your dormant masculine strength. Through His redemptive power He has transferred you out of the lineage of Adam and into His royal ancestry.[25]

It is His intention to train your warrior heart for knighthood. He has etched His kingdom-vision into the wall of your heart so that His mission can become your mission.[26] Through His redemption the stage is set for you to redeem. As He pours His life into you, His healing hands will begin mending your broken male image and reclaiming the honor of your manhood.

5

WHAT IS A MAN?

Hank eased off on the throttle of the outboard as we motored into the bay and approached the shoreline. The spit of land we were coming to was overgrown with briars, saplings, and weeds as tall as my head. Morning dew clung to the grasses along the bank, and my arch enemy, poison ivy, seemed well established in vines visible even from the boat.

As our momentum drifted us slowly toward a hard day of work, I stood up on the bow, prepared to jump to the bank and tie us off. Looking before I leaped, I spied a water moccasin coiled up at the water's edge catching the morning's first rays. I hopped over him and warned Hank, "Watch out for the moccasin just to your right."

"Oh, thanks. I've been nailed by them before and it is no fun."

Hank gathered up a handful from the assortment of rakes, hoes, swing blades, and axes we had carted over with us and handed them out to me. After two trips with handles going in every which direction, Hank crawled over the seats with the gas can, oil can, and chain saw. Returning from his fifth trip to the bottom of the boat with the water cooler in tow, he peered starboard at the gray-black, listless snake who was doing his best to be inconspicuous. "That's a big snake. Three feet I'll bet."

"Did you say you had been bitten by a water moccasin before?"

"Yeah. Three times actually." Hank's head was buried under the stern seat as he tried to extract the watermelon we had brought with us. Not being able to see his face, I wasn't sure if he was pulling my leg or telling me the truth.

Producing the melon and a fish stringer, Hank smiled an uncharacteristic smile and handed them to me. His implication was clear: Figure some way to secure the watermelon to the bank with the fish stringer so the watermelon won't float away before our afternoon break.

Hank's hair matched the three-day growth of his beard, which matched the hair covering most of his body, all of which was going every-which-ways.

"So what did you do?" I asked.

"About what?"

"About getting bitten by a water moccasin."

"Oh, just laid around mainly. I felt bad for three or four days, but then I began to get over it."

"So, you never went to the doctor or anything?"

"Nope. The way I figured it, when one of our dogs got bit they laid up under the porch for a few days—swelled up some—and then came out none the worse for the wear about three days later. Since I'm bigger than the dog I figured the same plan would work for me. And it did, 'cause here I am."

"Can't argue with that, Hank. You're here alright, and so am I, and so is a whole bunch of stuff we've got to clear out by dinner time."

Our Principle Ally

Consider it for a minute: Is Hank a real man? Is he the kind of guy we are all aiming to be like? If so, let's go a step further: What will make Hank a Christian man? Teaching Sunday School?

Being an elder or a deacon? Going to Promise Keepers every year? Being in an accountability group?

Although these are worthy pursuits, the more of these thoughts that are thrown onto the table, the more confusing the issue is to sort through. In fact, the more we try to define masculinity by describing a stack of stereotypical male performances, the more I get the idea we are sorting through the wrong stack of stuff. We will not find the wealth and strength of manhood by establishing new parameters for male behavior—and getting bitten by a water moccasin won't help prove your manhood either.

"Masculine" is not something you do, and neither is being a Christian man a role you perform. Masculine is what you *are*. Christian is *who God made you when you became a believer*. Therefore, being a Christian man is not a play you act out. It is living according to who God made you to be. Being a Christian man means living your life the same way Jesus Christ lived His.

It is time to rethink our ideas. Masculinity has nothing to do with appearance, job, hobbies, accomplishments, family, Christian activity, or how many times you have been bitten by poisonous snakes. Masculine is who and what you are. The challenge is not to *become* masculine. As Paul said in 1 Corinthians, it is time for us to "act like men [and] be strong."

Contrary to Hollywood's image and society's belief, men do not function optimally as lone wolves. Friends are essential. Allies treasured. Loyalty among men is a badge of honor. A man who demonstrates dependability in the face of difficulty builds security in his friends. The man who sells his ally to make a buck or advance his own interests is a man who has missed an essential aspect of manhood.

Every man knows you don't go to the woods by yourself; you don't hunt alone. Dangers—both real and perceived—prowl about seeking to destroy you. In your heart you know that if your masculinity is diminished, your world takes a loss at a fundamental level. Conquering the challenges that come into your life are battles that must be fought and won. There is no cost too high, no cause more noble. But in the face of any challenge a solitary man is a vulnerable man. Who will stand by you and fight against these forces threatening your manhood and working to undermine your masculine role?

Jesus Christ, the perfect man, lives within you and wants to express Himself through you. Being a Christian man is agreeing with God that you are a man, and therefore are masculine, and then diligently developing a close relationship with your Heavenly Father where you depend upon Him as your life and strength. It is this man—Jesus, the Son of God—who is your ally.

We Are Warriors

Gary Smalley and John Trent say, "Men have always been hunters, warriors, and adventurers. The call of a challenge—whether it is picking up a sword to join the Crusades, setting sail in a small boat across the Atlantic, or tackling Mount Everest 'because it is there'—is something God has wired within a man."[27]

What does that quote mean? Thinking through it myself, Vietnam wasn't quite the same as the Crusades, but I signed up for the draft when I arrived at age 18 even though I didn't have to serve. I looked at the pictures and read the article in *National Geographic* about Thor Heyerdahl sailing the oceans at great personal risk aboard his small raft, Kon-Tiki, and stood in awe of his accomplishments. I read Jon Krakauer's book, *Into Thin Air,* about the tragedy on Mount Everest in 1996 as John Hall's team reached for the summit and got bushwhacked by a rogue blizzard of hurricane proportions. But to do these things myself because God wired me that way as a man? I'm not sure I can relate.

I spend most of my day in front of a computer monitor or participating in meetings in a conference room. This is hardly the lifestyle of a warrior, although now that I think about it, the review I read when shopping for my notebook computer was entitled, "Reconnaissance Report by a Road Warrior." The only hunting I do is when Dianne sends me to the grocery for canned blueberries in light syrup. Adventurer? I have a friend in Georgia, Scott Brittin, who wants me to go spelunking with him, but I haven't gotten there yet. Regarding owning a sword, I don't, but I'm thinking about it now that I've seen "Zorro" at the theater. But I'm not into wearing the mask like he did. A nondescript uniform with epaulets and boots seems out of line for the president of a ministry, doesn't it? A sword with a nice gold chain fastened under the epaulet might be a nice touch, although I will have to modify the seat in my VW to accommodate the scabbard. Perhaps a short sword worn under my cape would be more appropriate.

Let's face it: In the traditional sense of the definition, I am not a warrior. But if, by the words, "Men are warriors," we mean they go out at great personal sacrifice to make the world a place where others can become all they are destined to be without the threat of having that process jeopardized by evil, then I do identify with being a warrior. By definition, I do that every day, and so do you. It doesn't have anything to do with getting shot at or standing on the heaving fore deck of a 13-meter sail boat wrestling with the spinnaker. It is about an attitude I have, and a commitment I have made, enabling me to provide for my family, protect my kids, and make sure my employees get a fair shake and my buddy has everything he needs for his family camping trip to Big Bend.

Being a warrior means a man lives his life in such a way that those around him are exposed to Jesus Christ. This encompasses playing ball with his son, getting to know the young buck wanting to take his daughter to the sophomore dance, and spending time shopping with his wife for just the right color of wicker patio furniture. Simply stated, a warrior lives like the Lord Jesus.

In the final analysis, I agree with Smalley and Trent: God *has* placed the heart of a warrior in the chest of every man. "Protector," and "provider" are etched into the DNA of men by the Creator of man. Life in any era is an adventure, and when I ponder God's calling for men, it causes me to want to stick my chest out, set my jaw, and declare, "Yes! I am a warrior with a noble calling. My Ally has vowed by His sacred honor to never desert me. As brothers-in-arms, we are ready for what faces us."

When Paul says in 1 Corinthians 16:13, "Act like men, be strong," I believe there are two essential elements indicative of masculinity and strength. The first is courage—courage to trust Christ, to believe what He says about your manhood versus how you feel, courage to depend upon Him, courage to be a seeker of God's heart. It takes courage to be a warrior loyal to the mission God engraved on your heart.

The second essential element of masculinity is resolve. This means making a decision to exhibit courage and not wavering from that commitment. It is resolve that sets your mind on what God says about you as a man instead of what you have learned, resolve to be undeterred in your tasks as a man, and resolve to stay focused on depending upon Christ to live His life through you. This resolve brings a man's destiny within reach.

The Destiny of a Warrior

There are six things a man's destiny hinges upon. First, a man knows his *story* is a struggle between right and wrong, and he is the potential hero. But he is engaged in a battle, the weapons are spiritual warfare, and the stakes are for who is worthy to be Lord based upon his allegiance to either God or Satan. A man's *story* is written by the choices he makes.

God chooses to love, call Himself love, refer to us as the ones He loves, and commit Himself to us without reservation. Satan chooses to accuse God, cast aspersion upon His character, and tempt us to live independently and reign as lord of our own lives.

By choosing to accept his sinful suggestions we offer the devil the opportunity to make a bid for the throne of God. His logic is this: If we—the men created in His image, and the ones whom God loves—will not depend upon Him, opting instead to run our own lives, how could it possibly be feasible for Him to reign over all creation? Satan's plan is to war against God by undermining a man's determination to depend upon his Heavenly Father. A man knows there is much more at stake than meets the eye.

Second, a man's destiny is to know his *strength* is discovered through dependence upon Christ, not his determination as a man. "True manhood is resourced in Jesus Christ," Jack Hayford says. "He is the only salvation for a battered or ambiguous male identity, and He's the provider of substance to bring definition to your manhood and mine."[28]

Third, a man's *source* is God. He must learn to become dependent on his Heavenly Father's sufficiency. It is not enough for a man to recognize his strength comes from depending upon Christ, he must know what his Heavenly Father thinks of him as a man. In order for a man to step into the remaining aspects of his masculine destiny, he must know God has destined him, equipped him, and blessed him. Manhood flows from who I am as a man, and who I am flows from the resource of my Heavenly Father.

The fourth aspect of a man's destiny is knowing our *significance* is anchored in Christ, not the techniques each of us have developed for getting our needs met our own way. Jesus Christ knew two things: He knew who He was and He knew He was loved by His Father. A man must know these same two things. If he does not, he will never be a secure corner post. A man—like a corner post—is only as strong as his anchor.

Fifth, no one is more insecure than a solitary, lonely man. A man's *security* is in Christ and with other men. A secure man is transparent and confident. And a secure man is strong, shares his heart, and puts his life on display knowing that by modeling secure masculinity he positions other men to step into the security he enjoys.

Finally, the sixth aspect of a man's destiny is for him to realize his *station* as a man is to assume responsibility for his redemptive role. Rather than emulate Adam's failure, a man must call upon the strength of the Lord to live and express a life of redemption rather than independence.

The Responsibility of a Warrior

If we look at manhood this way, it becomes clear the primary responsibility of a man is to build a deep, dependent relationship with his Heavenly Father. This *defines* his masculinity and shapes his self-concept—the shaping of a man is foundational to everything God is trying to accomplish. He wants to pass His family name to us, mature us, and as our Heavenly Father, He wants to bless us as His sons and His friends.

It is the responsibility of a man to build close relationships with other men—to march together, stand together, fight together, and work together. Men trust each other, depend upon one another, and respect each other. Men spar together, argue together, debate together, and then lock arms and depend upon each other to make them better men, more resolute in knowing their Heavenly Father. A man who will not pass the test of dependable, loyal friendship is suspect when circumstances become challenging. If a man trusts another man to look out for his blind side, depends upon him to help him through difficult situations, or calls upon him for counsel and consolation when life is dark, then that man carries responsibility for his friend's trust. For a man this is an honor and a sacred trust.

> Friendships not only reflect the man, but they can make
> him what he is. They form him. They decide his depth, his
> qualities, his skills and his destiny, for we're told, "He who

walks with wise men will be wise, but the companion of fools will be destroyed" (Proverbs 13:20).[29]

It is the responsibility of a man to bless his family and friends, realizing no one else can take his place or assume this privilege in the lives of those closest to him. His words, his touch, his encouragement, and his approval are indispensable to those most important to him. Through his blessing a man senses the capacity he has to draw out of his children, his wife, and his friends their potential to love, care, share, serve, and ultimately offer themselves as vehicles for redemption and friendship. His security with his station in life models security for them in their station.

Ultimately this positions a man for the greatest, most profound responsibility he has: to pass the mantle of masculinity. As a man becomes secure in his manhood, it is his privilege, duty, and honor to ensure the strength of masculinity is passed to the next generation.

Fundamentally, the way in which a man lives his life reflects to all observers how God wishes them to relate to Him. If a man lives a life of self-service, self-reliance, dishonor, and indecision, he models disdain and disregard for his relationship to God. If a man understands his strength comes from depending upon his Heavenly Father and models a life of service, courage, and resolve, he fulfills his destiny and carries out his responsibility to pass the mantle of masculinity effectively. A man living in this fashion is a true warrior allied with the King of kings.

Untouchable Strength

I was visiting a friend in Waterloo, Iowa, who collects tractors. But not just any old tractors. He collects only the best, which according to him are John Deeres. I don't think I ever saw Ralph in a pair of overalls that didn't have some John Deere green and yellow paint on them.

In keeping with the occasion and the spring day, I wore my Carhartt overalls, a flannel shirt, work boots, stuffed my leather gloves in my back pocket, and wore my Hampshire hog "gimme" hat. ("Gimme" is a southern expression for free. For example, it might be said, "Jimmy down at the feed store gimme this hat for buying a pickup load of hog feed." It is a fact the most common cause of marital discord among southern couples is disagreement about where the man keeps his gimme hats.)

The hundred-foot-long barn smelled of diesel and dirt, and was lined on both sides with tractors of all models and sorts. Ralph carried on a running commentary about which tractor he had gotten where, and what he had done to restore it. How any one person can know so much about all those different pieces of machinery, I will never know. I have enough trouble keeping my bicycle running right, let alone 50 or 60 tractors and their corresponding implements.

Ralph's favorite tractor was a 1929 Model D. I'm sure there must have been some part somewhere that wasn't iron, but except for the belt, I couldn't see it. Even the steering wheel was iron. It had no tires, just iron wheels with iron spokes and iron treads.

Ralph opened a petcock on the side of the engine in order to relieve some compression before trying to start the tractor. He then turned the flywheel to kick the two-cylinder engine into action. On the second spin of the flywheel, the engine pounded to life, its two cylinders popping and spewing raw fire eighteen inches out of its unmuffled exhaust pipe. It was impossible to yell above the noise of the exploding, fire-belching cylinders.

Reverting to hand signals and brief demonstrations, Ralph instructed me on how to engage the belt on the flywheel and drive the Model D. I pulled on my leather gloves, stood astride the differential of the transmission, braced my legs against the iron seat, and pulled back on the iron lever to engage the drive mechanism.

Belching fire and rumbling slowly across the dirt and gravel on the barn floor, the iron beast lurched forward. Using both hands and leverage from my shoulders and legs, I turned the steering wheel to point the tractor toward the barn door. As Ralph snapped my picture I thought to myself, *"You know, my wife Dianne could not drive this machine; she isn't strong enough."*

I found it amusing that that particular thought would come to me while I was driving the Model D, but it points to the fact men like to get in touch with physical strength because it helps them define inner strength. Typically, men don't understand strength intuitively, they do better if it is demonstrated.

While all men struggle to lay hold of what it means to be a "strong man," the man whose dad was absent may grapple laboriously with what masculine strength is. First of all, this understanding doesn't come naturally. Second, he can't say he has seen male strength demonstrated by a role model, and men understand strength better if it is demonstrated. Smalley and Trent say,

"Some of us had such poor models in our fathers or mothers (or both) that we've been left to piece together a puzzle without getting to see the picture on the box."[30]

There are lots of ways for a man to be absent: He can work all the time, or simply be busy; he can be quiet and not make himself known; he can die; he can be a perfectionist and isolate himself, striving for the right way to do everything; he can be passive; he can be undisciplined and let his impulsiveness sabotage the discipline relationships require; he can be harsh and gruff and in so doing isolate himself from anyone wanting to be around him; he can abandon his family through divorce. The point is this: As men try to assess whether or not they saw strength demonstrated for them by their dad or other male role models, there are myriad factors that could have circumvented God's intended plan for illustrating masculine strength. If there is no standard establishing what masculine strength is, how are men supposed to know if they are strong or not?

The voice of society is clear regarding a man's strength. There isn't much room for a man to operate in between being viewed as chauvinistic and being viewed as a bumbling idiot that women and children put up with. "It's a man thing," has come to mean irrational and inane. Somewhere in between these two extremes is a narrow point of balance defined as appropriate, masculine strength. But to a man this balance-point is often so narrow or fluctuating it is beyond his ability to state with confidence, "I am a strong man." Getting in touch with physical strength often helps a man feel he understands the elusive notion of inner strength.

Men want to be respected as strong men. For a guy to believe his strength has engendered and inspired loyalty makes him feel worthwhile, necessary, and valuable. A man who believes he is a strong man believes the world would be a poorer place without him. It is a man's strength that fortifies him to face life's battles. His strength helps him believe he is needed.

This being the case, when men wrestle to define their strength, or have doubts as to whether or not they are strong men, they lose confidence in their masculinity. An insecure man may act out, withdraw, overcompensate, or hide behind a poker face and a life philosophy which says, "Never let them see you sweat." And yet, when asked what characterizes a man, most people mention strength. Women find security in it. Boys glory in it, model themselves after it, and even mythologize it: "Dad, I told Dennis you could whip his dad. Could you Dad? In a fight, could you whip Mr. Johnson?" Men gauge their masculinity by it. They may even enjoy the mythology their son fantasizes—"Son, I would not fight Mr. Johnson. We are friends." But secretly, while continuing to read the evening paper, he thinks to himself, "*I wonder if I could take Rip Johnson out. He's a big man...but if I had to, I bet I could.*"

Women and children seek it. Men seek it. The world seeks it. All value it, debate it, and strive to find it. Can all men be strong, or is strength only for a few?

Act Like Men

"Act like men, be strong," the apostle Paul says. One thing about Brother Paul, he is emphatic. There is no mincing around. Straight to the point—Boom! "Act like men, be strong." But just between you and me, since Paul isn't in the room, *what does he mean?*

Let's work backward. When he writes, "be strong," Paul is stating a fact and combining it with an exhortation. In other words, "since you are strong, act like it." Men are strong, so don't be otherwise.

Paul is not exhorting us to go buy memberships at the gym and start lifting weights. It is true that one aspect of men is they are typically stronger than women, which is purely a principle of body design and physical mechanics, but this is not the strength

Paul is talking about. Physical strength is not the determining factor of whether a man is masculine or not—if it were, we could make ourselves men by going to the gym. We could have a contest like the Olympics to determine who was the best man. But once a guy gets to about age 35, he begins losing his masculinity. For those males with physical limitations, any hope of being masculine would be a pipe dream. Forget it!

No, if masculinity is based upon physical prowess, then it is a cruel hoax and an elusive dream. Paul's words "be strong" are hogwash. And yet this is almost the definitive standard foisted upon society as to what makes a real man. The movies, TV, and the locker room all blatantly hold up a standard of masculinity based upon physical attributes.

The results of this mistaken masculine paradigm are all around us. Insecure males exhibit macho complexes and masculine hang ups. Men all over the world force their sons to behave like they wish they could have behaved as young men. If you haven't noticed this, take a trip to a little league ballpark and watch the dads instead of the game. You will observe men reliving their youth vicariously through their sons, clinging desperately to a definition of masculinity the progressing years are stealing away from them.

We talked earlier about cultures where masculinity has completely lost its identity. Alcoholism, spouse and child abuse, neglect, abandonment, and vice are rampant in those societies as men try to grapple with a degenerating definition of masculinity, a definition of masculine strength confused by the loss of traditional male roles. And with all of this going on around us, Paul writes, "be strong." He does not say, "become strong," as if to convey working at it in order to accomplish the goal of strength. He speaks of strength as in existence now, indicative of who men are currently, and exhorts us to act like who we are—strong men.

The good news in this verse is that masculine strength is indicative of us as males. You do not *become* strong, you *are* strong. This offers a great deal of hope for most men, and relieves the burden for all of us. For those who have given up on masculinity due to age, physical limitations, sexual dysfunction, or some other obstacle, these two simple words from Paul are cause for great hope. For those working desperately to hold onto masculine strength, the pressure is off. You do not have to find ways to prove yourself. You are free to be who you are: a strong man.

If you are like me, you are probably saying, "It is great news that I am strong simply because I am a male, but I'm not sure how this works once I close this book and head out the front door to live my life." Think about the first part of Paul's comment—and "act like men." In other words, you are a strong man, so act like it. Two questions come to mind immediately: How do men act? And isn't acting simply a game of pretending—a nice word for hypocrisy?

If I dressed up like a woman and walked down the street, you would say, "That guy is acting like something he is not: a woman." My behavior would be hypocrisy in the purest sense of the word. On the other hand, if I dress up like a man and march down the street, you don't think anything about it. I'm acting like who I am. I may not feel like a man, may have an inferiority complex or an identity crisis, but this has no bearing on who I am. I am a man. Period. Regardless of what you were taught, how you feel, what the women's movement says, how Hollywood defines masculinity, how you feel sexually, what the latest commercials are portraying, what Mom and Dad said to you, or what the guys used to say about you on the playground, you are a man. Act like it.

Acting contrary to how you feel is not an accurate definition for hypocrisy. A hypocrite pretends to be something he is not. The man who does not feel masculine but acts like a man anyway is portraying who he is—and that is not hypocrisy, that's courage.

Along with Brother Paul, hitch up your pants, set your jaw, and with determination say, "I believe what Paul wrote in God's Word, and I am determined to trust Him to show me how to be what I already am."

CODY'S STORY

Robert Bly writes, "Only men can initiate men, as only women can initiate women. Women can change the embryo to a boy, but only a man can change the boy to a man."[31] Men need other men, and they need to do things with other men in order to understand what men do. Men struggle with vague intuitions, the place where women excel. We fare much better if we are together, demonstrating and living our masculinity. It is my observation that quite often when women are together they talk, but when men are with each other, they are simply together. When men are shoulder-to-shoulder it is more than a social event—they are being men and learning about their masculinity.

A few years ago I ran across a young man named Cody who needed a masculine presence in his life. I looked around to find someone to help him, only to realize I was the man for the job. In the imperfect world in which we live, Cody's story lacks many of the fundamentals God intends for a young man to have, but for a time Cody and I experienced life together.

Watching Masculinity at Work

The old John Deere belched a little black smoke, laboring mildly to pull the creosote eight-by-eight from its spot at the corner of the fence. The old posts needed tearing out…more or less.

I've been guilty of hunting for logs to drag and fields to plow, looking for an excuse to be on a tractor and always disappointed when the last row was done and the final roll of hay was up by the barn. But today there was a reason for the fence and its condemned posts. This day there was a reason for being on the tractor. Tragedy had me working.

Years earlier, a dad stood before his wife and son and told them he was leaving to find fulfillment in the arms of another woman. Just why he skipped out is not important; the point is he abandoned his boy, and that's where I entered the picture. The boy's name was Cody, and he and my dog Katy were best buddies. I don't know who loved whom the most, but I can assure you the feelings were mutual. Some sort of magic exists between a boy and a dog, and Cody's joy with Katy was the genesis of my relationship with him.

It didn't take a graduate degree to read in Cody's brown eyes the rejection he felt from his dad. I hurt for the boy, and I spent more than one night sitting by the wood stove wondering what I could do to help. In what turned out to be a revelation to me— and not knowing what else to do—I asked Cody if he'd come to the farm and spend the day with Katy and me. I fretted over the time as it approached. Pray as I would, inspiration for something profound to say that might ease his pain eluded me, and any creative ideas for a bang-up slap-happy time avoided me altogether. So when the day finally arrived and Cody showed up, I settled for something I'd enjoy in hopes he'd enjoy it too.

So it was we found ourselves smelling of creosote, inhaling diesel fumes, and admiring the power of John Deere's hydraulic lift. Any way you cut it, a chain is cantankerous to work with, but Cody and I had a good time lashing the posts with the heavy strand of looped steel and hooking it onto John's implement arms. The green beast extracted the posts with such ease that neither Cody nor I could help but grab the old uprights ourselves from time to time just to be sure we didn't possess something of John Deere's might. Our admiration grew.

It didn't take long to pull the posts and work through the other tasks I'd planned for the tractor, Cody, Katy, and myself... so we finished the afternoon down at the creek. (After all, what boy's day could end any better than being around the therapy of cool water?) We climbed down the bank, descending the stairstep roots, scrambling here and there for solid ground. We chased a water snake, caught a couple of crawfish, skipped a few stones, and topped things off sitting under a canopy of hardwoods listening to a ripple gurgle toward the big pool around the bend.

There were other days when Cody came over, each of them similar to the last: nothing necessarily profound, no magic in the air, not even anything exceptional—we just spent time together. I remember being especially busy one day with some really boring stuff, so Katy and Cody took off on their own. I tracked them down later, holed up together in a fort made of hay bales. Even though Cody had been on his own part of the day, I was close and that was good enough. Cody sensed he hadn't been abandoned even though my physical presence was elsewhere.

Learning Masculinity

Only a few months after that first day on the tractor, it was evident something had clicked in Cody—I had filled a crucial void. I received a Father's Day card signed simply, "I love you, Cody."

Men have difficulty articulating the inner emotion without referencing the outer performance. That's why it is critical for men to be with other men. At the time I did not realize what I was providing for Cody. In fact, he probably did a finer job of articulating it than I did when he sent me the Father's Day card. He knew he had gained something critically important, realized it had something to do with a father's job description, and sent me a card to say thanks.

It used to be that boys watched men in order to learn masculinity. Neither the men nor the boys realized this is what was transpiring, they probably attributed it to pragmatism—"I need help in the field son, and you're big enough to do the job. Come on. You're with me from now on." Or, maybe it was said, "Son, one of these days you will inherit the family business, just as I did from my father. We have built our customer base on integrity, honesty, hard work, and a superior product. Today, you will become my apprentice and I will groom you to carry on the family tradition."

While the boy was busy hauling water for the plow-mules or sweeping the floor in the shop, he was taking special note of how his dad handled the mules or negotiated with a most-important customer. The son observed how his dad carried himself, how he sweat, the way he loved, how he expressed his passions, talked of his wife, laughed, handled his anger, solved problems, how he prayed and read his Bible, talked of the pastor, and how he relaxed. He watched what happened when his dad met another man, how they shook hands, how they talked, where they stood, what they did with their hands, how they solved their conflicts, and how they made eye contact. He compared his dad's beard to the other man's, compared his dad's arms to the other man's, and thought to himself, *"I think my dad's hat has more character than Mr. Pannel's. I want my hat to look like Dad's."*

Dad was a role model, but he was much more than that. He was the purveyor of masculinity. He was the repository of manhood, the seat of maleness. When the boy thought of virility, robustness, vigor, power, valor, gallantry, fearlessness, nerve, and grit, he thought of his dad. This is the way God intended boys to be acquainted with masculinity. He intended for the boy to say, "I want to be like my dad," and for there to be honor in that statement. Ultimately, God wanted to make a comparison for the boy between Himself and the boy's earthly father.

Luke tells the story of Jesus and His parents going to Jerusalem to celebrate the Passover when He was twelve (2:41-52). This was about the age when Jewish boys began learning their father's trade. For Jesus this meant joining Joseph in the carpentry shop. But if you recall the story, Jesus gets left in Jerusalem and it is three days before his frantic parents find him sitting in the temple talking with the religious teachers. The irony of this story in Luke's Gospel occurs when His overwrought parents find Him and His mother says, "Child, why have you treated us this way? We have been terrified trying to find you!"

Jesus responds, "Why have you been looking for Me? Didn't you know I had to be tending to the things of My Father?"

The Bible politely says neither Mary nor Joseph understood what Jesus was talking about. His father's business was carpentry, and therein is the irony. It was time for Jesus to enter the realm of manhood by spending time with the men, and the men expected this to occur. In fact, they initiated it when a boy reached twelve. On the surface, it was an apprenticeship to learn a trade, but at a deeper level, it was about learning to be a man.

Men march together, ride together, stand together, and boys learn masculinity by being with, and observing, men behaving like men. If a man is isolated, his strength is jeopardized, and if a boy is isolated his sense of masculinity is jeopardized. A doubt rises deep in his soul that he is ill-equipped to identify or deal with.

If a boy can't see a man up close, masculinity never acquires a face, and although he learns to physically stick his chest out, he has his doubts as to whether there is really anything in there. The temptation to prove to himself there is something masculine inside becomes very compelling. But he is hard-pressed to formulate a scheme other desperate men have not already tried: power, women, authority, money, intimidation, dominance, isolation, or success.

Such a man lives by desperate hope rather than confident strength. He is a man who feels like an insecure little boy desperately looking for his father. If this man represents a corner post, we should prepare ourselves for a weak and shoddy fence row.

TWO ACES, TWO STRIKES

Dianne and I were going out for the evening. While she applied her finishing touches, I sat down in the den with the flipper to see what the TV had to offer. We do not have cable, so I only had twenty-three channels to chose from, and I settled in rather contentedly on a "Gunsmoke" rerun. There is always the danger of getting hooked on the .story line, but there is little danger of being emotionally stranded. After all, Matt Dillon has yet to die in one of those episodes, and Festus is still riding the same mule. Besides, those shows where they kill the mule and hang the hero aren't my kind of entertainment.

Because I tuned in forty minutes late, I have no idea what predicament Matt, Doc, Festus, Miss Kitty, and Newly were working their way through between commercials. Whatever it was, it called for Miss Kitty to have a high-stakes poker game in the Long Branch with some hapless bad guys and their boss-with-all-the-brains. They were killing time, waiting for the Marshall to walk into their insidious trap about ten minutes before the top of the hour. In the meantime, Miss Kitty was cleaning them out—and psyching them out—at the poker table with marked cards and two aces up her sleeve.

I hate to tell you this, but Dianne appeared looking great about a quarter to the hour and as a result I cannot tell you whether Matt is OK or not. I clicked the power button on the flipper and left with my woman for a night out on the town. But, I have been thinking about those two aces Miss Kitty had up her sleeve.

The Ladies' Aces

I realize this was just a "Gunsmoke" rerun, but whether it is Miss Kitty playing high-stakes poker on TV or real interpersonal relationships, women tend to have two aces up their sleeve. As a matter of fact, in a little girl's quest to become feminine, it is like she has this two-ace advantage almost from the delivery room. She is *verbal* and she is *intuitive,* and in interpersonal relationships, these two aces stand her in better stead than a man's ability to fold up a road map correctly.

Rather quickly, a little lady will conclude that Mom is the appropriate role model to help her become feminine and enter the world of womanhood. And she and her mom talk. They fill the air with words, words, and more words. If words made you wealthy, most women would be gazillionaires. They talk about everything. They even talk about nothing. In fact guys, here is some important inside information: Dianne tells me lots of public places—like churches and restaurants—even have areas set aside in the lady's room where they can sit and talk. (I'm not sure why restaurants do this, because I have timed Dianne and it takes just as long for her to go to the lady's room with her friends at the burger place as it does at the nice places with the couch in the restroom. Seems to me the owners could have saved the money for the couch and put one of those nice cases in the men's room to hold the front page of the paper and sports section.)

Women communicate constantly, and not just with words. Women touch and hug, cry together, and hold hands. They even communicate via the air or the water or something—something the dictionary calls intuition. They can say the wrong thing, or say nothing at all, and still be on the same wave length.

For example, on the fourth of July, Dianne and I always go with our friend, Dorothy, to the fireworks display over the Trinity River in Fort Worth. Dorothy is a ball to be with, and from year to year I remember more about the time with Dorothy and Dianne than I do about the fireworks. We take wieners, pop, chips, chocolate chip cookies, and all the traditional Independence Day fare, then drive to the Tandy Center parking lot by the river, set our lawn chairs up in the back of the pickup truck, and settle in for the celebration along with the rest of Fort Worth and America.

Last year, as I was driving toward the river, we were all three scrunched into the front seat of my truck, and Dorothy and Dianne were talking about a shop where one of their mutual friends had found some cute clothes. Well, they talked and they talked and they talked. They sited landmarks and intersections trying to be sure they had the same shop in mind. I happened to know where the shop was, because it is two doors down from "World of Blades"—a truly interesting knife store. As I listened to their directions, Dianne's locators were ten or twelve blocks north of the shop and Dorothy's were six or eight to the east, when suddenly they announced, in unison, "Oh yes! I know where that is! They have the cutest outfits this time of year."

I couldn't stand it. I interrupted their discussion and said, "Wait a minute. How do you know you've been there? You are sixteen blocks apart."

But somehow they knew—and they were talking about the same shop. That's intuition. When a lady says, "I don't know how I know, I just know," that is intuition, and she is often right. Women have this intuitive ace that enables them to stay in the relationship game. When words fail them, intuition kicks in and they go right on communicating.

A Man's Strikes

It is without a doubt a difficult trip for a little girl to navigate through adolescence and arrive safely at womanhood, but she has a verbal ace and an intuitive ace she can play as needed. She and her mom—and the other women around her—talk. And when words fail them, they communicate intuitively.

On the other hand, when a boy shows up on the planet, he has two strikes against him. He is neither verbal nor intuitive—and neither are his dad or his friends. Even a cursory evaluation of boys and girls will reveal that girls talk while boys make noises.

On summer trips to visit my grandparents, I would spend a fair amount of time with my cousin, Leslie. I remember thinking how disadvantaged poor Leslie Gail was because she could not make a decent bomb sound, gun shot, car engine, or strafing plane. I actually felt sorry for her having no recourse but to play house with Ken and Barbie while I was enjoying the finer points of how dirt clods exploded in front of my entrenched GI Joe army man with the scar on his face. While she changed Ken from his beach wear to his tuxedo, and dreamed of Ken and Barbie's date, I was rolling around outside in the grass identifying with my GI Joe's predicament in the dirt clod war raining down upon him.

For all of the verbiage exchanged between a mother and a daughter, as a general rule there is precious little verbal exchange between a boy and his father. While the boy is busy emulating the noises of guns, planes, cars, and automobiles, the dad is busy answering questions with grunts, hums, and nods. When boys and men do communicate verbally, it is often instructive, punctuated with short, sometimes terse, sentences: "Stand with your feet shoulder-width apart. Bend a little at the waist. Choke-up on the bat just a bit. Right elbow up. Keep your eye on the ball. Step straight ahead when you swing. Let me see you try. No! Step straight ahead. Again. That's better. Elbow up. OK. Under it that time. Don't dip your shoulder down. Here you go. Better. Again."

On top of that, when left to fill in the verbal gaps, a typical boy does not have the advantage of intuition. Masculine understanding is usually systematic, logical, and precise. It is not that a man is incapable of understanding subtleties or implications, but in a conversation like Dianne and Dorothy were having about directions to the dress shop, a man will most likely be lost by…oh, about sixteen blocks.

Moving from boyhood to manhood is a tedious and fragile task. While little girls approach their journey with two effective, navigational aids, boys start from an inherent deficit. Little girls begin from a position of strength, but boys start from a place of weakness. Certainly girls are dependent upon their mothers and other influential females in their quest to become feminine, but if they miss something in the process, they have their intuitive abilities to fall back on. On the other hand, boys are heavily dependent upon their fathers and influential men to demonstrate masculinity for them as they move from boyhood toward manhood. If this process is interrupted through the father's absence, divorce, indifference, passivity, or anything else that separates father from son, the boy will flounder and the unanswered questions pertaining to manhood will begin to haunt him. There is no substitute for the presence of an influential man in the life of a boy. Left to himself, a boy will grow to look like a man, but if he is to truly understand manhood, he must have the consistent influence of a real man in his life.

The passage from boyhood to manhood is one that begins in weakness and progresses through dependence. In that statement resides the great secret of a man's strength—strength is discovered through dependence.

As a boy traverses toward manhood, he is dependent upon his father to demonstrate masculinity and eventually welcome him into the world of men. If this occurs as God intends, the boy will probably be hard-pressed to articulate what has occurred or how he got where he was going, but he will exemplify masculinity and the strength of a man. The fundamental resource necessary to take his stand against the evils that assault him and anchor himself as a corner post will be undeniable. But even more profound, the boy will have an internalized, demonstrated understanding of how to depend upon his Heavenly Father. He will have learned this by being dependent upon his earthly father and watching how his dad depended upon God.

That is the divine plan: Through weakness and dependence, God's strength is demonstrated in men. We said earlier that one of the first things most folks think of when they think of a man is strength. Herein is the source of a man's great strength—dependence on God.

It has nothing to do with physical strength, sexual prowess, or accomplishments. Strength is demonstrated through a man's determination to live now the way he was taught to while progressing from boyhood to manhood by depending upon his Heavenly Father.

In 2 Corinthians 12:9-10, Paul writes, "And He has said, 'My grace is sufficient for you, for power is perfected in weakness.' Most gladly, therefore, I will rather boast about my weaknesses, that the power of Christ may dwell in me. Therefore I am well content with weaknesses, with insults, with distresses, with persecutions, with difficulties, for Christ's sake, for when I am weak, then I am strong."

When I am weak, then I am strong. It's perfect. The course for a man to become strong is the course he has been navigating since birth. God made a boy weak so he could learn how to let God be strong through him. Not only is a man a protector, provider, and warrior, he is a living demonstration of the way God wants to relate to the world.

The radicals assert men are no longer necessary. Feminism espouses women can do everything men can do. But if men are no longer needed, who will demonstrate how to live in a place of weakness? Who will exemplify true strength through dependence?

Who? There is no one else to do that if men do not! A man's strength is discovered and demonstrated through dependence. This contribution to the world is indispensable, and no one but a man can perpetuate it. Not a woman. Not a girl. Not a boy. No one. Only a man can do this, and a man knows he must be prepared to lay his life down to ensure this responsibility is carried out successfully.

> And what more shall I say? For time will fail me if I tell of Gideon, Barak, Samson, Jephthah, of David and Samuel and the prophets, who by faith conquered kingdoms, performed acts of righteousness, obtained promises, shut the mouths of lions, quenched the power of fire, escaped the edge of the sword, from weakness were made strong, became mighty in war, put foreign armies to flight.[32]

These men were heroes by any standard. The verses themselves allude to amazing feats, and it is some of the most fascinating reading in the Bible. But there in the middle of the stuff movies are made from, just after the part about escaping the edge of the sword, and just before the part about becoming mighty in war, is that characteristic common to all of these men: "from weakness were made strong."

It is this dependence that anchors a man as a corner post. If you are set in Christ, the Rock, you are anchored. If you are depending upon Him as your life, you are anchored. If you are relying upon Him as your strength, you are anchored. If you are not, you have no strength.

How Much Could Jesus Do?

Resolving to "do better" is not an appropriate response to the challenges before us. Certainly we have to make a decision to do what needs doing—but our Heavenly Father is not interested in our best effort, at least not initially. He is interested in us depending upon Him, implementing the lesson of our childhood, being transparent with our approach to life with Him as our strength. That sort of effort begins with a determination to depend upon Christ to express Himself through us.

This is not a mysterious theological concept I dug out of a dusty tome, but a reality of life. It is not one iota different from the way Jesus lived during His tenure on earth. If you think about it, the Lord talked about this a great deal. He said He could do nothing Himself (John 5:19). He couldn't pass judgment (John 5:30), He couldn't speak (John 8:28, 14:10), He couldn't come from heaven to earth (John 8:42), and in fact, even though He was God in an earthsuit, Jesus said He couldn't speak a commandment (John 12:49).

Now let me ask you a question: Could Jesus literally not do anything by Himself? Could He not walk outside and get the morning paper by Himself? Could He not tie His hair back in a pony tail and trim His beard by Himself? Could He not put on His work sandals or drive a peg into a hole with a hammer in His carpentry shop by Himself?

Of course He could, but He didn't. Jesus said He couldn't do anything independently of His Father because in so doing He would irrevocably destroy the mission of redemption His Father had sent Him to accomplish. Jesus could not sin and still be the sinless Lamb of God, slain from the foundation of the world. The determined choice Christ made, demonstrated, and articulated was to obey and depend on His Father. The attitude with which He approached life is the attitude with which I am supposed to approach life.

Certainly it is my feet walking out to the front yard for the paper, my hands shaving my face, tying my shoes, turning on my computer, and feeding my face. But my attitude must be reliance upon the strength of Christ in me. If I fall short of that standard, I depend upon my own resources and declare God unnecessary for that occasion. If I live life under the delusion that my personal male strength is a true picture of masculinity, I conduct myself no differently than Adam did in the Garden of Eden. I destine myself, and those around me, to live under the scourge of a man who is failing in his task as a man.

A strong man, a redemptive man, a courageous man, a secure man, a well-anchored man depends upon the strength of his Father. Such a man does not approach life from any other perspective. As he pads across the floor to the bathroom first thing in the morning, a strong man says, "Father, I'm depending on You today."

Men who depend upon their Heavenly Father establish themselves as a benchmark of strength. They position themselves to demonstrate true masculinity. In this way, a man offers his life as an instrument of redemption, laying it down so the boys who follow in his footsteps, the girls learning what makes men tick, and the women who relish the security of a man's strength can realize what God wishes to communicate to them by the manner in which he lives his life.

Dependence upon his father is what characterizes a boy's journey to manhood, and dependence upon his Heavenly Father is what characterizes a man's strength.

DREAMS OF YESTERYEAR

A long, snaking abrasion appeared on the face of the Oklahoma earth as the single bottom plow gouged its way along under the weight of the old Indian and the unsteady pull of a war-pony converted to plow horse. A single feather dangled at the quill from the gray braid of the warrior. One to match was tied by a leather thong to the horse's mane. Bent over his plow and looking at the wrong end of his horse, dreams of yesteryear filled the aging warrior's mind. He stopped for a moment to reminisce of prairie grass, buffalo, and a horizon beckoning to him from the back of his pony. Now, only a furrow called to him at the end of his reservation plot. Looking into a sky of clouds, the west wind etched the figment of his mind. Once again he was bareback on his pony feeling the horse's heat on his thighs and their fluid unity galloping in the midst of the buffalo herd. Feathers, hair, horse, rider, and bison moving in symphonic motion. There was life. There was calling. How was a dark gash in the earth supposed to replace this memory of identity? Could he find himself in spite of this plow and live again in the meaning he found with dreams of yesterday?

Few paintings move me as much as the one I've just described by William R. Leigh, which hangs at the Woolaroc Museum in northeastern Oklahoma. With oil and canvas words, the artist has portrayed a condition of the heart. How will this old plains warrior pass on the song of his soul while behind a plow instead of astride his horse? His awkwardness is so consuming it must surely be evident to the young ones who look to him for the treasures that will build their identities. How will the young men pass the skills of manhood to their children if all they have are worn stories of yesterday?

Men are a complex mix of extremes. Treat a man poorly if you are not close to his heart and he will shrug you off. But tread on his dreams and you wound him profoundly. Disrespect him from a distance and he pities you, but question his worth as one who has access to his soul and you possess the power to jeopardize his sense of identity. He is tough, resilient, driving, and independent, but molded through close, timely dependence upon his father and older mentors. Disturb his routine and he flexes. Disrupt the delicate transition from boyhood to manhood and he suffers immeasurably.

The Delicate Mission

Boys become men by watching men. Boys become men by standing close to men. They become men by observing things only men know. Effective manhood is a ritual passed from generation to generation with precious few spoken instructions. Passing the torch of manhood is a fragile, tedious task. If the rite of passage is successfully completed, the man is like an oak—strong and hard. His shade and influence will bless all who are fortunate enough to lean on him and rest under his canopy. However, if the divine plan is disrupted and no mentor steps in to pick up the responsibility, the boy will grow to look like a man but will be faced with the unenviable, treacherous task of finding true manhood by accident or with the help of Hollywood's role models. It is God's design that a man's shoulders be capable of carrying a considerable load of responsibility. The way a boy gets there is a delicate mission.

Is this some divine curse? Certainly not! It is a *blessing*. Within every man is a constant reminder of what God intended the Christian life to be. In weakness and fragility the boy depended upon his father to provide his strength. As a man, blessed with strength, there is humility in knowing it is not my strength but that which I was blessed with by my father. Is there a more accurate portrait of the Christian life? While the temptation remains constant to declare myself strong and independent, real fulfillment comes in recognizing that it is Christ's strength in me and through me making me what I am.

But what if in the process of gaining manhood an inconsistent representation of Christianity is given? If the things of Christ are given secondary priority, Christ Himself is depicted as nothing more than a figure of the faith, and "religion" is taught in place of personal relationship, what will become of the most important priority in a man's life? The boy will grow strong with the inherent strength of a man, but be hardened against the humble acknowledgement of his dependence upon Christ as his life. While dancing the dance of life, he will struggle to make reality of the true dream of manhood God wired into him.

Men—Christian men, true men—are made, not born. Men fashioned as God intended when He first thought of men are not conversationalized into manhood; they are shown, guided, tutored, and mentored.

Admitting Our Need for Christ

There was a time some years ago when the passage from boyhood to manhood was more clearly marked, when men were more confident in what manhood meant, and life in general

guided men as they passed their blessing on to the next generation. Things aren't quite as stable today. Our fast-paced, high-
demand lifestyle can encroach on a man's time. It is no longer a
given that sons will follow in their father's professional footsteps.
Education is supposed to help a boy decide what to do with his
life. Character, dignity, honor, and integrity are not valued as
highly as force, opportunity, avarice, and cunning in making a
man powerful. The reverence for and submission to divine
absolutes has been replaced by a relative ethic. Everything is
judged by how it relates to the individual, and is given value
based upon whether it is beneficial or pragmatic. Self-sacrifice, at
least on society's list, occurs only if it serves self. The meaning of
"Christian man" has been fogged over, secularized, and abused.

It isn't any mystery why our bookstores are suddenly stock-
ing their shelves with books on men. It shouldn't be a surprise to
hear of men's groups forming all across the nation to offer support
to marooned males. Neither should we wonder why our young
men are growing more violent and acting out through their
music, art, language, and lifestyle. Why Christianity has been
tossed aside isn't really much of a riddle, given it has been strip-
ped of esteem, value, and force. Men are in trouble. They feel it
deep in their souls. They are aware of their trouble, but are not
skilled at acknowledging weakness or verbalizing fear. Inwardly
they sense their calling and purpose, but outwardly they are confused, frustrated, lonely, and longing for true manhood.

We know by now a man's strength is not the stuff of young
bucks flexing their physical muscles. As Bly puts it, "By the time
a man is thirty-five he knows that the images of the right man, the
tough man, the true man which he received in high school do
not work in life."[33] Neither is a Christian man a smiling, som-
berly reverent, nonemotional, nonconfronting, and nontrans-
parent individual who is very different at home and work than he
is at church.

It is a cop-out to claim perpetual bondage to something less than true manhood because you were thwarted in your passage from boy to man. It is also a cop-out to deny you have been hurt by being deprived of a healthy transition to manhood. You are never so weak, or bound, or deprived that Christ is not sufficient. To acquiesce in denial is not representative of the masculine strength Christ wants to forge and demonstrate in you and through you.

There is no doubt the deficit a man feels within himself is the result of perplexing and painful issues. No one would deny chiseling off the rough edges of one's character is a difficult, painful task. However, the great message of God is that He is our security, strength, and refuge. He is our Father, and there is not enough bondage or weakness to challenge His sufficiency. Fundamentally a man needs security, strength, refuge, and identity. Foundationally, God promises to supply all of these needs.

Perhaps the heaviest decision a man will ever make is to subdue his will and admit his need for Christ. For the man who struggles within, confused about his masculinity, such a decision is perhaps obvious. However, to the man skilled in the rituals of maleness and confident in his strength and power, such an admission of weakness and need might be viewed as unnecessary. Which of these two men has the greatest male need? The latter, without question. He has missed the most basic lesson of what makes a male a man—he is dependent on a father. It is essential that a man not forget the humble lesson of boyhood. We are all dependent upon our fathers. To assume an adult has any less need for reliance upon *the Father* is a tragic error in understanding the real strength of a man.

Life no longer needs men to ride war-ponies across the great plains in search of buffalo herds. Life does require, and always will, that a man's inner world reflect the God-given dreams of what masculinity is really all about. The drive for masculinity, inserted by God into a man's genetic code is as present in today's high-tech world as it was in the day of single-bottom plows. If plows and hunts and horses made males into men, then today's computers would offer little hope. And if men could be developed alone, by mere mortals, then manhood would not require God's sufficiency.

You Can Depend on Me

I am a cyclist. Not like Miguel Indurain, Bernard Hinault, Greg LeMond, or Eddy Merckx are cyclists, but a cyclist in that I ride seriously and with determination. I have spent a fair chunk of change buying bicycles and cycling equipment, and when I go to bed at night, I often fall asleep reading *Bicycling* magazine or with a dog-eared copy of the *Colorado Cyclist* draped across my chest.

Whizzing along at 20 miles per hour, I do not dare take my eyes off the rear hub of my riding partner's wheel for more than a split second. My front wheel follows behind his rear wheel by six or eight inches in order to ride in the slip-stream of his body and let his draft pull me forward. The principle is the same as in car racing—drafting reduces drag, saves fuel, and is energy efficient. Of course, riding a bicycle at 20 miles per hour is a little different than driving a car at 200, but those guys are surrounded by a roll-bar and cage of reinforced steel. Meanwhile, I am sitting on top of a 19-pound piece of aluminum alloy with the wind in my face.

After he pulls me along for a few minutes, my partner moves to the side, slows his pace just a bit, and allows me to ride past him while maintaining my speed and cadence. As I slip by, he accelerates and pulls up to my rear wheel. My slip-stream then pulls him along, providing a much-needed rest before it is his turn to "pull" again.

With several riders, this becomes a sort of cycling "dance." Each rider drafts the person in front of him, working his way up the line until he assumes the point and creates a draft for those behind him. Like a gaggle of geese minus one side of the "V," the cyclists race forward working in rotation.

Crouching over the drops of his handlebars, the lead rider determines a predictable line to ride and does not detour from this course. He glances at his cycle computer and makes a mental note of his speed. Unless the road is hilly, he works to maintain a steady and unrelenting pace. His cadence does not vary substantially. As one cyclist writes, "The most essential group riding skill is to be steady and predictable."[34]

It is critical the lead rider not become so engrossed in coping with the wind or being the lead rider that he fails to keep his eyes on the road before him. A hole, broken glass, a storm drain, or road junk are his responsibility to see and predictably guide the group around. Everyone else is looking at the person's wheel in front of him and depending on the point man to look out for them. A sudden jerk by the man in the lead will most likely result in a catastrophe behind him. He cannot afford to do anything stupid.

Not long ago I was riding with a group south of Fort Worth. We were ten or eleven miles south of town, riding a black top road splitting the prairie in two. A fast group of riders came past me in a tight pack, the whirring of their gears and tires had a throbbing, rhythmical sound as they articulated their way through the slower cyclists. The lead rider reached for his water bottle, his shoulder dipped a few inches, and his head twisted ever-so-slightly. Inadvertently, he swerved. Tires touched. Thirteen riders piled in on top of him. Hundreds of dollars worth of high-tech equipment and tanned, lycra-clad bodies entangled and twisted into a grating, scraping, cursing, bleeding mess on the asphalt roadway. The lead rider's water bottle rolled down the center stripe of the county road.

Predictability, dependability, steadiness, perseverance, and steadfast endurance—the marks of a dependable point man. A reliable riding partner doesn't do anything stupid.

A man knows strength is like this. Strength is not a burst of energy. It is not the final push you give a car you are trying to get started. A man's strength is steady, predictable, and dependable. When tension is taken against the well-anchored corner post, when the cattle rub against it, when a storm assails against it, someone runs into it, the post doesn't move. It stands. A man's strength is synonymous with steadfast endurance.

Strength does not quit. It finishes the task in spite of any difficulty, stays on course in spite of any hazard, and maintains pace in spite of any confrontation.

This is not to say that a man's strength is unbending and rigid, or that he has to live within the same small box all his life. But strength undergirds the way a man approaches life. Those on the road know what to expect from him. He is dependable and isn't going to do anything stupid. This type of strength in a man breeds security in those riding through life with him, and it creates security in the man himself. Because he is secure in his strength, he can say to others, "Come ride with me."

The lead rider who jumps up to the front of the pack and takes off like a shot, leaving the group behind, misses the point of working together. A leader takes the people who follow with him as he advances. That is the security of strength.

Raul and Salo

Raul and Salo, who are 11 and 8 respectively, lived across the street from Dianne and me for several years. Their father was an alcoholic who spent his time downing beers and watching television. The boys spent their time at our house. The only thing they didn't do was sleep at our place, though they did that on a couple occasions.

One Friday night we invited Raul, Salo, and one of their cousins to stay the night with us. We ate pizza, watched a movie, and then showed each of them to their beds. After the lights were out, they all three decided to sleep in one double bed because they were scared of Dianne's doll collection. It had to do with some movie they had seen about a doll that ate people or something. Figuring that was how they probably slept at home, we didn't worry about it too much.

Raul and Salo had four or five run-down old bicycles they rode hard and put away wet. I was forever mixing and matching parts, replacing bearings, tightening handlebars, and straightening seats. And I'll bet I patched a thousand flat tires—give or take a few.

After about the tenth flat, I decided it would be better to teach them to fix a flat than for me to fix it for them. I'm a slow learner, but bicycle flats, like automobile flats, happen at the most inopportune times. It was always easier to fix them myself than take the time to show the boys how. Why turn a ten-minute job into a 45-minute job? "Besides," I reasoned, "this will be the *last* flat I'll fix for a long time."

And then I caught the vision: Fixing flats is part of passing the mantle of masculinity. It is one part of a man's strength a boy can identify with. It's an aspect of being a corner post. And it was one way I could take Raul and Salo into the adult male world.

Salo was a little young and much too uncoordinated for flat-fixing, but Raul was in his bicycle-flat-fixing prime. There was grass to be mowed, weeds to be pulled, trees to be trimmed, a garage to sweep out, and two cars to maintain, but the next day Raul and Salo showed up with a flat. I spent as much time as Salo could endure working on his bike with him—about five minutes—and then encouraged Raul to help me with the task at hand. It was an invitation he could not refuse.

As I stretched the bicycle tube over the vise and instructed him how to clean the tube and prepare it for the patch, his small hands wrapped around the tube next to mine and his black hair pressed against my beard as he positioned his face directly over the vise to get a good look and not miss a single detail. I had fixed enough flats by this time that I didn't need to see what I was doing.

The other things waiting for me paled in their importance. Raul and I—and even Salo to some extent—were connecting at a level far deeper than simply working together. More was taking place than the accomplishment of a task. By talking with him, standing beside him, taking him into the issue at hand at the level I dealt with it, Raul glimpsed the world of a man. The resonance of masculinity began sounding in his soul. Being close to me, Raul felt my physical strength, smelled my masculine scent, brushed against my hairy arm, and felt the pull of his hair against my beard. His hands got dirty like mine. He felt my warmth on the wrench when I handed it to him. In a word, he felt my strength—the strength of a man.

Fixing flats was not the only time Raul and Salo entered my masculine world. We sat on the driveway in the evening, worked in the yard together, ate together at McDonald's, and watched the Cowboys on "Monday Night Football." They listened to me pray and saw me read my Bible. They heard me apologize when I made a mistake, felt my arms around them when I greeted them, and heard my words when they went home at night—"I love you Raul. I love you Salo. See you tomorrow."

Talking with young men, taking them with you, letting them stand close to you—these are ways in which a strong man exhibits his strength to a dependent boy. It's how he pulls those around him close enough to see the true source of his strength: his dependence upon his Heavenly Father. Only a strong man lives this way. Only a man secure in his standing with his Father lets people this close to him.

When a man exhibits this kind of strength, he is laying his life on the examination table, sharing himself in hopes that through his example others will find life. This is the cause for which a man is uniquely equipped. It is the role of a warrior—his code of honor. It is the way a man demonstrates the masculine role of redeemer. By sharing his life, a man declares, "Yes, it is true my forefather, Adam, failed in his task as a redeemer, protector, provider, and warrior. But I refuse to follow in his footsteps. I am determined to trust my Heavenly Father to live His life through me and demonstrate His strength. He has made me a strong man. I choose to act like it. I do not wish to take rank with those poor spirits who neither enjoy much nor suffer much because they live in the gray twilight of masculine insecurity. I choose to depend upon Him and demonstrate strength."

The man who shares himself helps boys grow into manhood.

SIT DOWN, EULA

Stories are like windows to the soul. Through their transparent reflections, our hearts connect, memories emerge, identification occurs, our lives entwine, and meaning dawns. Stories enable us to pull back the curtains and share the stuff of our lives as peers. Ken Gire writes, "Stories protect us from the small-town perils of our own parochial way of looking at things."[35]

In the story that follows—courtesy of the Fort Worth *Star-Telegram*—Frank Perkins opens the window of his soul in a story rich with the stuff of life. Through events he mentions only in passing, his family was fractured by tragedy but bonded together with what some would call scars. I think Frank would call it love. His definition of family is generous and big—big enough to accommodate the twists and turns life takes. The extraordinary events shaping this forty-six-year-old memory are indicative of how boys pass from boyhood to manhood. Frank does a masterful job of articulating the role older men play in the lives of boys on the threshold of manhood:[36]

> I can still feel my most memorable Christmas gift in my
> hands, even though the gift was given to me 46 years ago.

It was not fancy, nor expensive, nor wrapped in luxurious paper and bows. Instead, it was given as if it were my right to have it, and that made it even more special to me.

The gift was given by my stepgrandfather, a man whom I regarded with a mixture of puzzlement and awe and who I thought considered me of no consequence whatever.

It was 1946. The war was over and my father had returned safely from the U.S. Navy. It was Christmas Eve, and as usual, we would spend it and Christmas Day with my step-mother's parents in their small sharecropper's farmhouse in Denton County between Little Elm and Frisco.

I was 12. The awkward age between childhood and the teen years. This particular Christmas, I especially felt the awk-wardness. I was still too young to be included in my dad and stepuncle's Christmas Eve quail hunt that had become a family tradition.

I was too old to gather with my stepmother, her sisters and my stepgrandmother in the kitchen and peel potatoes and carrots and listen to the gossip and wisecracks that crackled like summer lightning from this remarkably verbal group.

"Get out from under our feet, boy, go find something to read or to do outside," my stepmother said to me as I hung around the small kitchen, already crowded with just my stepmother, her mother, and two sisters.

A third sister and her husband would be coming that night after getting off work in Dallas.

There was nothing to do outside. I already had read every-thing in the small house, including the quaint *Farmer's Almanac*. There was no one my age, no neighbor kids, just North Texas blackland farm in dead of winter, with a cold rain blowing down from the north over the small forgotten cemetery on a hill just north of the house. The temperature was dropping from the already chilly 40 degrees. I went out anyway and headed for the barn.

In the barn were a pair of mules, a wagon and my stepgrand-father, a tall, spare, monosyllabic man who had spoken perhaps 50 words to me when my widowed dad married his youngest daughter. She had nursed him [my dad] back to health after the car wreck that had widowed him and left him with a year old baby to raise.

The old man called my dad and his other in-laws by name, but he never called me anything but "boy."

He was engaged in one of his favorite chores, grooming his two fine Missouri mules, his most prized possessions and in the opinion of the whittlers and spitters at Dick Riddle's General Store in Little Elm, the finest pair of mules in Denton County.

The mules stood quietly as he moved between them in the straw-filled stable, brushing their mouse-gray coats to a satiny sheen with a curry comb; rubbing their velvety noses and scratching behind those long, expressive ears.

He was thin and to me, mysterious. His clear blue eyes were friendly, but a sweeping white mustache, the tips stained by the tobacco he chewed, and his silence made him a figure of awe. Like the other members of his family, I called him "Our Papa."

In the summer, when I made extended visits to the farm, I would ride with him for hours on a plow pulled by those two mules.

It was a fantastic, yet strangely speechless experience. The clean animal smell of the warm mules, the creaking of the harness as they shouldered the plow through the rich black land; nests of baby mice dug up by the plow blade, rabbits wheeling away in flight almost from under the mules' hooves.

None of these things were everyday events to me; they did not occur in the sophistication of Fort Worth.

Despite all these wonders, he spoke not a word, although I would yell and point and shout, "Look, Our Papa, a rabbit!" I would turn and see only a small smile under his tobacco-stained mustache. Then he would acknowledge my attempt to share with him what I thought was a wondrous occurrence with a slight nod.

When he would spy something interesting I had missed, he would click his tongue in a softer sound than the whip-like snap he used when he was starting his mules.

Hearing the click, I knew he had something important to reveal and would look at him. He would raise a finger and point and I would follow the line of the finger and see another wondrous sight such as a neighbor's mare with her newborn foal or a huge red-tailed hawk sitting on a distant fence post.

I thought he was a remarkable man because of his silence. He would sit in his favorite rocker in front of the Christmas tree, his presents neatly stacked nearby, while his sons, daughters, daughters-in-law and grandchildren all talked, laughed, joked and jabbered at the top of their lungs because my stepgrandmother, Our Mama, was deaf as a post.

Through all that loud, raucous fun, he would sit and smile, his eyes dancing, and say not a word. A particularly barbed sally would draw a short "Ha" from him.

But now it was supper time on Christmas Eve so he put up the curry comb, and he and I wordlessly walked back from the barn into that warm kitchen for a supper of chicken-fried steak, mashed potatoes, preserved corn, pickled beets and hot biscuits.

Outside, the first ice began to form on the mud-slicked back roads as the temperature continued to fall. In the living room, my stepmother and her sisters kept up their gossiping while Our Papa read the newspaper and Our Mama fussed about what was keeping Aunt Eula and Uncle Clarence. We all decided it was that darned old Dallas traffic.

I remember going to bed and to sleep amid the murmur of those voices and the chiming of the old Seth Thomas clock on the mantel.

Three hours later, at midnight, the old man was shaking me gently.

"Get up, boy. I need your help. Dress warm and get a heavy coat," and then he was gone.

Wonderingly, because those were the longest three sentences he had ever spoken to me, I got up, pulled on my warmest clothes and a new fleece-lined jacket and went into the kitchen.

The women were all there, sitting around the table in their robes and housecoats. A pot of coffee boiled on the stove.

"A neighbor came by and told us Aunt Eula and Uncle Clarence ran off the iced-up road up by the store," one of them explained. "Our Papa wants you to go with him in the wagon to get them."

About that time I heard the jingling of the mules' harnesses and went outside and climbed up beside the old man, bundled in a shapeless mackinaw on the wagon seat. He gave that special "giddyap" click of his tongue and we were off into the chillingly cold, dark night.

The icy ground cracked and crunched under the iron-rimmed wheels of the wagon as we negotiated the turn onto the Frisco road and headed toward the store, about two miles away.

Once the mules were lined out straight, there came my special little click from his lips. I looked over at him and suddenly he pushed the reins at me.

"Here," he said, "you drive 'em."

Amazed and wondering, I took the reins. It was like grabbing electricity. The power of the mules, slugging into their harness pulled me to my feet and thrilled me to my core. Our Papa grabbed the tail of my new jacket and pulled me back into the seat. "Stay with 'em, boy," he said.

By then the mules had figured out something was haywire. Even in the blackness, I could see those remarkably expressive ears whipping back and forth, semaphoring confusion and question about who had the reins.

The reins sagged a bit in my hand, that awful pull easing. Then came that whipcrack tongue click of his followed by a rare "Hi, mules!" from Our Papa. Instantly, the four ears snapped into the "alert" position and that awe-inspiring pull came back through the reins as they moved back into the harness and resumed their easy gaits.

I have never again had such a sense of power, or connection with the basic elements of that earth as I did at that moment. This was what men did. This was what being a man was all about: controlling intelligent, loyal beasts and moving to the rescue of your family in the dark of night.

Heady stuff. And I was being allowed a taste of it. The veil of the mysteries of adulthood had been pulled aside a bit.

And suddenly there was Aunt Eula and Uncle Clarence's 1939 Ford V-8, its streamlined nose buried in the ditch.

I pulled back on the reins and then died a thousand deaths as my voice cracked when I called out, "Whoa-a-a-a, mules!" There followed another semaphoring of mules' ears at the strange screech and the rather tentative tug on the reins, but they stopped.

My stepaunt and uncle, carrying their Christmas gifts, quickly climbed aboard the wagon and bundled in blankets and quilts sent by the women.

Then my stepgrandfather turned to me and said, "Get us home, boy."

I imitated his tongue click. It was a poor effort, but the ears wavered a time or two and then the beasts surged into the harness and we were moving toward the store a mile or so away where we could turn without risk of sliding off the now-deep frozen ruts into the ditch.

I was terrified about the turn. How did you do it? Then I remembered Our Papa's gnarled hands and how they worked to make those turns while plowing.

At the appointed time, I began the drill. It was almost too much for my aunt. She had already had the unsettling experience of winding up in a ditch that night and she wasn't quite up to sitting idly by while a nervous 12-year-old boy soloed at turning a wagon and two-mule hitch.

She stood up in the rear of the wagon and reached toward the reins. I was concentrating on the turn and was unaware of what was going on until the old man said in the sharpest tone I had ever heard him use: "Sit down, Eula."

Eula sat down.

A half-hour later we were back home and Eula was chattering away with her sisters and mother. Clarence had carried in the luggage and the gifts and the old man and I were unharnessing the mules: the first time I had ever been allowed to help with that chore.

My hands were still tingling with the feel of the vitality and power of those animals, transmitted back to me through those worn and patched leather reins.

We spent 10 more minutes wiping down the mules and then returned to the house where a still-jabbering family, now joined by my dad and other stepuncles back from the quail hunt, waited.

As we stepped up on the back porch, the old man put his hand on my shoulder and called me by my name for the first time.

"Good work, Frank."

That hour in a freezing open wagon, being given the responsibility for driving the finest pair of mules in Denton County to rescue relatives in need, was the finest Christmas gift anyone has ever given me.

YOUR FATHER'S BLESSING

12

I'm not sure when I began wondering about manhood, but I know it was before I became a man. For example, I was 9 when I discovered a BB gun under the Christmas tree with my name attached to the stock. I knew I was viewed even more responsibly when Dad handed me a .22 caliber rifle for my twelfth birthday. Landing my first job when I was in the fifth grade earned me plenty of spending money, a new bike, and a growing savings account. By the next year I was paying for half my school clothes, financing all my miscellaneous purchases, and saving for a car, but the ultimate achievement remained firmly out of sight.

Somewhere around eighth or ninth grade the question crossed my mind, "I wonder if you are considered a man when you get your driver's license?" It didn't take but a couple of years for me to realize an Oklahoma driver's license and having the whole town opened up to me and my red MG did nothing conclusive for my masculinity. Not only was the dream still out of sight, it seemed to be elusive as well.

"When do you get old enough to stop calling Mr. Ketch 'mister' and start calling him 'Bob'?" I mused. For me, this was the point at which I would know manhood had arrived.

Not to worry. I was sure that upon arrival at age 18 manhood would come to rest upon my broadening shoulders. After all, at 18 I could die for my country, vote, graduate, go to any movie I wanted, and drink beer if I chose to. The Vietnam War was still perking along, but the politicians were looking for a way out of it. Though the draft was in decline, the recruiters showed up nevertheless and offered to show me the world if I would sign on the dotted line. I was honored by their attention, but I had no real interest in the nuclear propulsion system of a submarine, applied avionics, or heavy artillery. So I stayed in school, studied the world, and continued to wonder about manhood.

I cut my long hair, grew a beard, paid my way through college, kissed a few girls, traveled some, and began thinking about a profession. The thought occurred that masculinity would settle upon me when I shook the president's hand as my college degree was conferred, but such was not the case. That's when I decided I had better hold off making a decision regarding my manhood until I garnered a second college degree. And so I waited another couple of years while I was completing my graduate studies and starting my own counseling practice to make a final determination about the elusive mantle of masculinity—manhood, and its bequeathal upon my head and shoulders.

Wouldn't you know it? I felt no different with two diplomas on my wall than I did with one. Consequently, I made an executive decision. One day, during a jog in the rain through the national cemetery across the street from my apartment, I bestowed manhood upon myself.

I took full responsibility for the failure. I figured I had missed it somewhere along the way, and I determined I had better get on with manhood since I had no doubt lost a great deal of time to my contemporaries. Although the honor was past due, I reasoned it was "Better late than never." And so I jogged home a man, from a run that began as a boy.

Choosing to Become a Man

The next step was the more difficult for me. Now that I had declared myself a man, I wondered what men my age did. There were those traditional things—chasing women, drinking hard, living recklessly—that I had neither the desire nor the physique to pursue. What was definitive manly behavior?

While I conducted further study, I returned to my original benchmark and determined to begin calling all men by their first names...unless they were doctors or had doctoral degrees. (In light of being a new man, this seemed only reasonable.)

Talk about a big decision! The next day I tried it on for a size: "Hi, Bob." What a funky feeling that generated! It was like I was being disrespectful to my elders. But I continued with determination, willing to feel unworthy and presumptuous rather than rescind my bequeathal of manhood upon myself.

Becoming a man is a confusing, disconcerting, and most of the time unceremonial metamorphosis. In fact, it is so bewildering that there are many men with graying temples who still feel like boys inside. There are desperate fathers God blesses with a boy to whom they try to prove their masculinity at the expense of their son. Or they are insecure enough about their escaping youth that they prove to themselves they haven't lost the proverbial step by competing against their child. Roger Rosenblatt, an editor-at-large for *Life* magazine said,

> I speak with authority as one of America's few 50-year-old basketball players, who at one time played competitive ball but who now confines his unusual game to his family. Perhaps it's too much to call my game a "game." On the court these days I move like a 1930s gangster in an aerobics class, dragging my legs in clumsy lateral patterns, flailing my arms without effect as if attempting to flag down a taxi in a blizzard.

> I am, as they say, pathetic. My "jump shot"—so called by me alone—consists of a general heaving upward of every part of my body but my feet.

My opponents are either my younger son, John (12), or my older, Carl (25). Carl plays with the quiet confidence of a man who can beat me every time. John plays with the quiet confidence of a boy who knows Carl's confidence is but a couple of years away.

When I play with the boys nowadays, I am, thanks to my physical inferiority, a better man—and a better father. I am no longer in competition with my children for childhood. To think! It took a mere 50 years to achieve this admirable maturity.

I don't think it was that much fun for Carl to know he had to beat my boyhood to earn his manhood.[37]

For many a man there has never been an occasion when his dad, grandfather, mentor, big brother, or the older man he looked up to welcomed him into the male world. There has never been a signal saying he has arrived at his destination. No man has ever said to him, "Congratulations! You made it. You are a man like me. Welcome!" No man has ever taken him to dinner, bought him a gift, given him a plaque, honored him at a banquet, thrown a party in his honor, or written him a letter. Nobody ever defined when boyhood ended and manhood began, and he is haunted by the doubts of this distinction.

In his best-selling book, *Iron John,* Robert Bly discusses how other cultures authenticate the passage from boyhood to manhood. As you would imagine, there are a whole variety of ceremonies, celebrations, and cultural events used to accomplish this all-important rite of passage. However, the most striking note of this research is not what other cultures do, but what western culture fails to do. There is no formal rite of passage, no defining moment, no authenticating task, no ceremonial blessing, no solemnization of manhood for the young men of our culture. *There is no point at which manhood is bestowed upon a boy.*

This failure generates insecurity in the hearts of men, and ultimately in the hearts of boys, girls, and women because men are not firmly anchored as the corner posts of society. Insecure men are desperate for acceptance, confused about their roles, intimidated about the problems they feel and can't articulate, and fearful they will not find a solution to any of the above. When men are insecure about their masculinity, the world suffers because there is no stability. There is nothing to gain a bearing from, nothing to stand beside, and nothing to start from. No benchmark. Simply put, an insecure man does not understand what true, masculine strength is. As a corner post, he wobbles at the top and wiggles at the bottom.

Moving from a boy to a strong man is a tedious process— after all, the two primary footings are weakness and dependence. Tinker with the process, impair it, belittle it, or undermine it and the passage from boyhood to manhood becomes bungled and plagued with masculine doubt.

Fumble!

I was sitting across the table from Martin Jacobsen, twenty-eight, an inch or two over six feet, 180 pounds, jet-black hair, with a four-year-old MBA that had garnered him a nice job making a large salary. He was married to Sylvia, a delightful lady nothing short of a class act, and by all I could tell, marriage was treating him right.

We discussed everything from mountain biking in Crested Butte to the project at work due on the tenth of the month, but eventually we wove our way to Martin's family. He grew up in a fine home filled with love. The bond between his brothers, his sister Julie, and himself was tight, but as he talked it became apparent his dad had dropped the ball in a few fundamental areas. For all the spoken love and affirmation, Martin's dad short-changed him by failing to share his time, personal thoughts, and attention. Other priorities got the best Mr. Jacobsen had to offer. While he instilled in Martin his moral convictions and commitment to integrity, his dad didn't share his life with him, didn't help Martin come to grips with manhood or masculinity, and now that age was creeping up to the back door, the prospects of Mr. Jacobsen making up for lost time dimmed with every conversation they had.

It didn't take a psychologist to recognize Martin's pain. He recounted the mistakes with a measure of ease, insight, and confidence, and it was just that attitude that caught me off guard. I said, "It sounds like your dad dropped the ball a few times while you were growing up."

"Yes, he did," Martin replied. "But that's not what bothers me. I've been fairly successful at letting his failures slip by. What I don't understand is, why won't he pick up the doggone ball?"

No doubt there are plenty of good reasons why Mr. Jacobsen did not pick up the ball. Perhaps he struggled with his own sense of masculinity and feared passing something less than ideal to Martin. Maybe no one had ever passed the mantle of masculinity to him so he felt inadequate to pass it to Martin. Nevertheless, Martin needed his dad to securely hand manhood to him with his blessing. He needed his dad to chart the course toward manhood and let him know he had made it, he was proud of him, and it was time for Martin to carry himself with all the honor, responsibility, and dignity inherent with manhood. All of his successes and failures aside, Martin needed his dad to pick up the most important ball in his life—manhood—and hand it off rather than leaving it lying on the ground as if it were of little importance.

The poignant and powerful aspect of Martin's story is that it points to the fundamental need a boy has and the primary responsibility a man carries. Physically, Martin didn't need anything from his dad. In fact, he wasn't even holding out for an apology. Martin knew in his heart—as all men know—the game of life called for him to be a man. He knew manhood was his destiny and he realized being a man was more than making big money, loving a woman, siring children, earning respect, and tapping into the world's power grid. While Martin could not articulate his need as I am doing in these paragraphs, in his heart he knew he needed something from his dad he had not gotten. Worse, what he needed most his dad neglected to give him.

Was manhood so unimportant the fumble was insignificant? Was this a haphazard transition, suitable for anyone to pick the ball up and do with it as he pleased? The failure seemed huge to Martin, but the fact the ball just lay on the ground created confusion—masculine confusion.

Within his question, "Why won't he pick up the doggone ball?" is also fear. Martin knew he was tapping into the great American dream of success. He was already tasting the best the world had to offer and knew in his heart there had to be something he was missing. If salary, accomplishment, recognition, and power were supposed to assuage the ache he felt inside and temper the masculine soul waiting to be fired in his heart, Martin feared all he had wasn't enough to supply what he needed.

He was ahead of a lot of men. Many guys don't recognize the hollow promises their pursuits offer them until much later in life. In his heart, Martin felt the fumbled ball had something to do with fulfilling his need, but the fact seemed almost not worth debating. Underneath his question, Martin was arguing a point: *If the blessing from Dad, the declaration that I've arrived at manhood, is so important, Dad would pick up the ball and hand it to me. There is some connection between this yearning in my soul and the blessing of my dad.*

I think of Martin's struggle as indicative of masculine insecurity. As you read this account of my lunch with Martin, you may or may not identify with the details of his life, but if your dad dropped the ball and left you confused about the nature of true manhood, you are asking the same question: "Why won't he just pick up the doggone ball?"

Men need to have manhood passed to them by a strong man. In God's wisdom, He designed that process to mirror His definition of true strength. As it is with a boy and his dad, so it is with a man and his Heavenly Father. This is the reflection God intended men to see. If the handoff does occur for a man, he probably won't be able to tell you what happened, but the result will be a man stationed in life, able to weather the storms, leaving an enduring legacy. A corner post will be set to site off of, to establish boundaries, to push and pull against; a corner post able to withstand the tension of the world. Such a man will know his strength is not his own, but that which he saw modeled during the transferal of the mantle of masculinity from his father. Starting with two strikes against him, he depended upon his father to take him from the weakness of boyhood to the strength of manhood. And now, following the model he learned as a boy, he is depending upon his Heavenly Father to exhibit real strength through him.

The magnificent thing is this: Whether your dad handed the ball of manhood to you in a definitive way, dropped it, forgot it, ignored it, or punted it over the infield bleachers, there is a blessing for you from your Heavenly Father. He has not, and will not, fumble the ball. Period. It is too important, His integrity too absolute, and His commitment to you too resolute. He will address your masculine insecurities.

Recovering the Fumble

Masculine doubt. Insecurity. Fear. All because the man who was carrying the ball dropped it and didn't recover his fumble. Dropping it is perhaps understandable, but not picking it up creates confusion.

Your dad may not have known any better, or maybe he didn't get the ball confidently handed off to him. Perhaps he doesn't care, doesn't do such things, is estranged toward you, is dead, or maybe you never even knew who your dad was. What now? You've read all of these pages and realize the fumbled ball is still lying in the dirt.

But, no. It is not. You need to look again.

It's not there. Someone picked it up. Your older brother, Jesus Christ, left the grandstands of heaven and sprinted across the open field of life's stadium, dived into the milieu of confusion, and recovered the lost ball. In sacrificing everything He possessed, Christ confirmed the importance of reclaiming what was fumbled. And once recovered, He didn't simply lie on the ground with it. He picked the ball up, tucked it securely under his arm, and sprinted toward the end zone to place it securely in the outstretched hands of His Father.

Now I want you to envision this with me: You are standing next to your Heavenly Father and your older brother at the beginning of what is left of your life's course. Before you are the best remnants life in the first Adam has to offer to you. The enemy taunts, claiming the Ones you are standing next to are not dependable. "Don't rest in their security," he shouts. "They are not worthy. Trust no one. Depend on no one except yourself. To do otherwise is weakness. You are the master of your fate, the captain of your soul." Satan's presence makes the air feel close and stale. Scattered corpses of the men who have failed in their tasks litter the course before you.

But you are standing beside your allies. Your older brother has His hair pulled back. His thick, black beard is well groomed but it curls and frizzes in the heavy atmosphere around Him. His arms and hands have not lost the definition they gained in the wood shop, and the nasty scars concealing the holes gouged by Roman spikes years ago are stretched between his wrists and palms. Your Father is unperturbed, calm compared to everything transpiring before you, but His thoughts are intense. His hands are massive, with distinctive veins much like Michelangelo portrayed them in his paintings. He does not simply hold the ball, He possesses it.

After taking time to assess the situation, your Heavenly Father moves a step toward you. He is close alongside, elbow to elbow, shoulder to shoulder. Gripping the ball with His left hand, He puts His right arm around your shoulder, places the ball against your chest firmly, and speaks these words directly to you:

"I'm proud of you son. In fact, you are My pride and joy. I don't know of anywhere in the universe I would rather be than here with you right now. This is an important day. I want you to know I believe in you and have confidence in you. I'm glad you are My son. As I have already demonstrated, there isn't anything I would not give in exchange for you.

"Your commitment to trust Me and depend upon Me makes Me proud to be your Father. Because of your commitment, I commit My strength to you. Together, we have a fabulous future before us, one we will look back upon not too many days from now and say, 'We were always on the road to victory.'

"Son, you are in My heart and I am in yours. I will never leave you without My strength. I love you beyond My infinite ability to verbalize. Today you are a man and I welcome you into the world of manhood with all of its joys, benefits, glories, and opportunities. I exhort you to be a strong man. Rely upon Me. Don't forget the lesson of dependence you learned as a boy.

"And now, may you always walk with a determined step, Christ-like character, unswerving integrity, and may your head be held high with the confidence of a man who knows he is a strong man. When you reach the end of your life's journey, may you say with conviction, 'I have run a good race, fought a good fight, lived life with passion, depended upon my Heavenly Father, and loved Him with all my heart.'

"Son, I have asked your older brother, Jesus, to go with you, to anchor you, to be a constant demonstration of how a strong man lives. And now, man to man, I hand this ball to you. Embrace it, hang on to it, and just as your older brother recovered Adam's fumble and redeemed you, look carefully for those whom you are to redeem. Wrap your arms around this ball in My strength, son, and I'll meet you both at the other end. This is My proclamation. You have My blessing."

13

BOYS TO MEN

Major Ian Thomas is an old brother who has wandered the globe preaching and teaching the great truths of God's Word ever since leaving the British armed services after WW II. Several years ago, the Major was teaching in a ministry I was working with closely. Since he was staying near our home, he put his feet under our table three times a day for breakfast, lunch, and dinner. Thomas is a delightful man who insists on making his point using a finger shot off to half a stub in the war. He speaks in rhythm and rhyme and is spellbinding with his ability to articulate God's desire for believers to depend upon Him absolutely.

Over the course of the week, the Major taught fantastic truths from God's Word. I took notes and thought about his messages during the day. Over lunch one day I asked the Major what was on tap for the evening session. My heart sank as he announced he was going to do his slide show. Watching someone else's pictures accompanied by copious commentary is not my idea of a good time. (In all honesty, the thought crossed my mind that we were going to see slides because the Major was out of sermon soap!)

I was wrong. Wrong about the slides and wrong about the Major's soap. The show was a pictorial history of the Torch-bearer's ministry the Major had founded. He is never without a young man who travels with him as his secretary and assistant, and the slide show depicted graphically what happens when a young man spends time with an influential, older man.

There were young men sent to the Major by their parents in hopes he could straighten them out. There were hitchhikers he had picked up, church kids, lost kids, English kids, German kids, American kids. You name them, they had traveled with the Major.

If he said it once, he said it ten times during the hour-long slide show: "If you take a boy, and wait long enough, he will become a man." I agree with the Major, but his statement short-changes his role in the lives of these boys. Left to himself, a boy will grow up to look like a man, but he won't know anything about manhood. That requires the involvement of an older man. Men initiate boys into the realm of manhood. Men demonstrate for boys what masculinity is and how men function. Keep in mind Robert Bly's words: "Women can change the embryo into a boy, but only men can change the boy into a man. The active intervention of the older men means that older men welcome the younger man into the ancient, mythologized, instinctive male world."[38]

Martin Jacobsen's dad is not the only dad who fumbled the ball. Men all over the world wrestle with questions related to masculine doubt and male insecurity. But regardless of whether your dad fumbled the ball or handed it off to you definitively, the point remains: Your Heavenly Father has placed His capable and determined hands on the ball, and while handing it off to you, He has blessed you as a man. He is proud to call you His friend and His son. The impact of this proclamation may not have taken effect emotionally, but the fact remains.

Not only is dependence upon his Heavenly Father the great secret of a man's masculine strength, dependency upon his Father is the source of a man's life. In other words, there is more to a man than strength. Emanating from his Father comes identity, belonging, reason, purpose, worth, and respect. A man who has an unshakable source for these commodities is a confident man.

Identity

Even if you were short-changed by your earthly dad, your Heavenly Father has blessed you as a man. And Christ, the ultimate example of true masculinity, intends to live life through you if you will work in concert with Him. He wants to run the course with you, in you, and through you. Paul pointed out in Colossians 1:27 that our hope of glory is Christ in us. And believe me, He doesn't live in me because He needs a place to hang out. He lives in me to express Himself through my life.

You are your Heavenly Father's son. Jesus Christ is your older brother. This would seem to be a pretty good sign that your identity crisis is over. Your Father has blessed you as a man, and Christ, the ultimate man, wants to exemplify manhood through you.

Think for a moment how Christ conducted Himself as a man. He was tender with the woman at the well, frank with Nicodemus, assertive with the money changers and Pharisees, forgiving to Peter who failed him, broken hearted at Lazarus' death, and longing for the companionship of His friends the night of His trial and crucifixion. Was He secure to be Himself? Sure He was!

Who are you? How do you behave? Do you have it within you to exhibit that level of security? Yes, you do. When your Heavenly Father blessed you and instructed your older brother to run the course of life with you, He made ample provision for you to behave like the man He recognizes you to be—a strong, secure man who understands how to depend on Him. This is your identity, and He is your source for living.

Belonging

One of my dad's friends said to me the other day, "No doubt about it. You are your father's son." This guy had in mind the sound of my voice and my sense of humor, and I am proud of the fact people recognize me as Bill Gillham's boy. There is no one else I would rather have as my dad.

But while my father has done a great job of being a dad, there are lots of men who cannot make the same declaration. In my case, we will celebrate Dad's seventy-first birthday before this book is printed. The clock is ticking. Whose son will I be when my dad dies? It is great to belong to the family of Bill Gillham, but belonging to the Gillham family is not enough to carry me through the challenges I face as a man.

No matter how well your dad did, or how poorly he did, your sense of belonging needs to be wrapped up in something more than your family name, the company you work for, the team you played for, the school you went to, the frat house you lived in, and the clubs of which you are a member. None of these will stand the test of time and none can provide the sense of belonging our Father intends you to have in Him.

My dad's friend spoke truth, he just didn't capitalize the "F" on father. I am my Father's son—my Heavenly Father says I am a member of His family and a citizen of heaven. As we have already established, Jesus Christ is my older brother. I walk in His triumph, according to 2 Corinthians 2:14. This means I am part of the family's victory parade and celebration. I am seated at my Father's right hand, the place of honor, and I belong there; I didn't get that seat by default. My Father put me there. Romans 8:17 tells me I am a joint heir with my older brother.

Let's talk about that "joint heir" benefit before we pass it off as another familiar passage of Scripture. I have three brothers: Mason, Will, and Wade. If upon the execution of my parent's will the four of us discover we are named as co-heirs, we will each inherit 25 percent of our parents' estate. On the other hand, if their will names us *joint* heirs, we each inherit the entire estate. When God stipulates through Paul we are joint heirs with Jesus Christ, he means we are heirs to everything our older brother is heir to. Your Heavenly Father makes Himself clear: You belong. Period. It is time for you to understand His perspective of you.

Meaning

You may be familiar with Norman Maclean's book, *A River Runs Through It*. As an avid fly fisherman and lover of good literature, I enjoyed both the novella and the movie. The story centers around two brothers and their father, a Presbyterian minister who loves to fish. The opening paragraph is a classic:

> In our family, there was no clear line between religion and fly fishing. We lived at the junction of great trout rivers in western Montana, and our father was a Presbyterian minister and a fly fisherman who tied his own flies and taught others. He told us about Christ's disciples being fishermen, and we were left to assume, as my brother and I did, that all first-class fishermen on the Sea of Galilee were fly fishermen and that John, the favorite, was a dry-fly fisherman.[39]

The author goes on to tell how he and his brother used to have to study *The Westminster Shorter Catechism* for an hour on Sunday afternoons before they could accompany their father for a walk in the hills prior to the evening service. Their dad would ask them only the first question in the catechism, "What is the chief end of man?" And they would answer from the catechism in unison, so one could carry on if the other forgot: "Man's chief end is to glorify God, and to enjoy Him forever." That answer always seemed to satisfy their father, and set the three of them free to go to the hills together.

"Man's chief end is to glorify God, and to enjoy Him forever." When God asks us to glorify Him, He is asking us to enjoy Him as well. As we enjoy Him, we glorify Him. When a man enjoys

God he demonstrates the vitality the Lord had in mind when He initiated a relationship with us. That brings glory to God. It says He is fun to be with, His redemption worked, man can have fellowship with Him, we are acceptable to Him, and He longs to be with us. The way a man conducts himself with his Heavenly Father exemplifies God's grace and sufficiency to his family, his friends, and his colleagues.

Our lives are not temporal, and our seventy-five or eighty years on this planet are not irrelevant to eternity. Whether I choose to act independently and live under the power of my own resources, or walk dependently relying upon the sufficiency of my Father to make me strong, I make a declaration filled with eternal meaning. How I live my life is not meaningless. As a man, my life is a benchmark, an eternal statement, a reflection of whether or not God should be relied upon, an indicator of whether He is everything He claims to be.

A lawyer once asked Jesus to identify the greatest commandment in the Law. He answered, "You shall love the Lord your God with all your heart, and with all your soul, and with all your mind" (Matthew 22:36-37). I think it is possible this was Christ's way of saying it is of utmost importance to enjoy God, knowing that if the listeners grasped the import of His statement and applied it to their lives, they would glorify Him in the process.

It is also significant that when Jesus was asked this question, He did not answer with the Great Commission or any of the performance-oriented commands of the Mosaic Law and rabbinical teachings. Christ knew if a man loved God and enjoyed his relationship with Him, he would glorify God with his life. A godly man is not to be defined by Christian performance, though behavior is important. A godly man is defined by Who he loves and enjoys, and Who loves and enjoys him. We all know men who are not believers yet live a more exemplary, Christ-like life than many Christians. There are lost men who are more loving than saved men, and non-Christians more moral than Christians.

If spiritual meaning is connected to performance, confusion will run rampant and the real issues surrounding eternal meaning and manhood will be clouded. Meaning in life is not fundamentally about performance, but about a relationship of love, enjoyment, and glory with God Himself.

Purpose

Fundamentally, *what* a man is doing in life is not nearly so important as *how* he is living his life. A strong man trusts his Father and relies upon Him. This dependent attitude positions a man to hear from God, and gives God the man's ear to direct him. God is interested in what a man does, but first and foremost He is interested in whether a man depends upon Him. He gets no glory from a man who produces moral, ethical, or religious behavior in his own strength. Such a production is a testimony to that individual's resolve and usually produces pride in personal strength—a temporal commodity. That man is deceived. A strong man understands the lesson he learned growing up: Strength comes through dependence upon the Father.

Men are uniquely qualified to share their source of strength. While women may be born with two aces up their sleeve—verbal acuity and intuition—they need to learn how to depend upon their Heavenly Father just like men do. The very things that assist them in their quest for femininity may hinder their ability to understand dependence. The fact that men are generally neither verbal nor intuitive actually positions them to understand true strength and demonstrate it for the women and children looking to them for leadership. What greater meaning in life could there possibly be than being called upon to enjoy God and accurately reflect our relationship with Him?

If men fall for the enemy's lie and think they are strong because they can run faster than a bullet, jump higher than a tall building, and stop a speeding locomotive in its tracks, they collaborate with the devil's quest to sit in God's chair. When men live independently, they declare God unworthy to run their lives. By trying to be strong themselves, men discredit God and lend credence to Satan's rebellious charge. Is it any wonder your life's course is a battleground? Is it surprising your feet must be anchored firmly in the rock of Jesus Christ if you are to stand secure? This is why your Heavenly Father instructs you to put on your armor (Ephesians 6:10-11) and to "gird up your loins like a man" (Job 38:3). The enemy is charging the throne of God, and he plans to come through your turf to get there. Brother, it matters how you live.

On the Team

I wish I could tell you I was a professional football player and you could see my bust on display in the Pro Football Hall of Fame in Canton, Ohio. But such is not the case. It became apparent in high school that I had better think of another way to earn a living than banking on my athletic abilities.

Toward the end of my playing days, the extent of my time on the field came during practice. I was second string and I played for a coach who put only the starters on the field—many of whom played both offense and defense. Occasionally, if he could run up the score, my coach would pull the first string and let some of the rest of us play. It didn't take long for me to lose interest in playing football and "retire."

As my last season of organized ball came to a close, I had the poignant experience of being on the team bus heading back to the locker room after a big win. I hadn't gotten to play. The cheerleaders were lined up beside the bus, yelling and sticking their pom-poms through the windows, horns were honking, the band was playing, and inside and outside the bus the school fight song was being sung—"Here we go Lions, here we go!" All around me the smell of sweat and grass and dirt filled the air as we inched our way toward the stadium gates. I sat in my seat, helmet in my lap, and thought, *"My uniform isn't dirty."* Try as I might, I couldn't feel part of a victory that didn't get my uniform dirty.

Manhood is not a game where some of us sit on the bench while superstars carry the day. There is no practice squad or second team. I used to tell people I played tailback, because every time I got near the field my coach would yell, "Gillham, get your tail back!" But this is not the case with God's team. Each of us is on the field, and each of us has the same opportunity to exhibit the strength of our position as a man. If we run the race, fight the fight, hold fast to the identity our Father has bequeathed to us, and with resolve determine to depend upon our Heavenly Father, we will share in the victory and glory in the fight song.

Whether the reality of this has sunk in or not, you are on the team. The Father has handed us the ball, blessed us, instructed our older brother to run the course with us, and taught us to depend upon Him as our strength. He is our source. According to Hebrews 12, the field is replete with the encouragement of those who have gone before us. We are not isolated, that's just the devil yelling nonsense. We march on a field fought over by the veterans of the faith. God's Book shares the stories of many strong men who believed Him. Who lived according to His strength and in light of the identity He conferred upon them. The Lord intends nothing short of the same for you and me.

Do you recall what the Father said to us when He blessed us? He said He has always shared the road to victory with us. Let's enjoy Him, reflect Him in our lives, and accept the identity, belonging, meaning, and purpose of what it means to be men. When the game is over, and time has tolled its final bell, we will share the ultimate victory of men in league with God Himself.

YOUR NET WORTH

14

Every man knows deep in his heart the family car ought to be a truck. This is part of the dementia that comes from all of the testosterone coursing through our bodies. There might be a wife, five kids, two dogs, a cat, and a bird in the family, with a two week driving vacation planned, but to a man it still makes perfect sense to have a truck for the family to ride around in. "No dear, you don't understand. It's amazing what you can put behind the seat if you get an extended cab. The bird will be fine in the back."

Let's say it is time to buy a new truck. You don't need to read and research—it's what you have been doing before you go to bed at night since you were in sixth grade. You are set. The fact is, a man is ready to go truck shopping on Saturday morning even if notified at midnight on Friday.

You walk onto the lot, go directly to the trucks, and stuff your hands—all but your thumbs—into your blue-jeans pockets (you wouldn't dream of going truck shopping in Bermuda shorts). Then you begin sauntering, leaning on tailgates, looking for the jack, counting the number of lug bolts used to hold the wheels on, making sure it comes with a full-size spare, eyeballing the ground clearance of the differential, and reading through the literature on gear ratios and other equally important information associated with good truck shopping.

At some point, you and the salesperson get down to the business of money. You dicker a bit, negotiate some, argue a little, bluff a tad, make a trip to the men's room, stare out the window, sigh, walk around the show room reading stickers, drink a can of pop, eat some popcorn, talk with three other guys, scrape your foot around on the floor some, and eventually agree on a sales price. Next you shake hands, push your hat back on your head, act indifferent (it's just a truck after all), sign a ream of papers, and finally arrive at the critical moment.

After everything is said and done, you slide a check for the agreed-upon price across the sales table and the salesperson slides the keys to your truck to you. At this point in time your check and the keys to the truck are equivalent in worth. They are equal in value. Your check is worth the keys to the new truck, and the keys to the new truck are worth your money.

The Value of a Man

Some time ago, God went shopping. He was looking for a man who would enjoy Him, love Him, and represent Him on Earth. Like any wise buyer, He was price conscious, but at the same time He was prepared to pay whatever was necessary to get what He really wanted.

As He looked around—"kicked a few tires," so to speak—He came to you, liked you, and decided you were the man He was looking for. He considered your cost against His available resources and decided He wouldn't be satisfied if He didn't buy you outright, on the spot. And so He did. The price tag on your head read, "$JESUS.00," and that is exactly what He paid, not a bit more, not a bit less.[40]

So I ask you: What are you worth? Go ahead, say it to yourself. In terms of value, *I am worth Jesus.* Furthermore, this transaction tells us about Jesus' worth—He is worth you. Jesus is worth you, and you are worth Jesus. In terms of value, God believes you and Christ are equivalent. I'm not saying you are Jesus, or that you are equal to Jesus. Jesus is the Lord and you are you, one *the* Son of God and the other *a* son of God, but both equivalent in value based upon the price paid by the Buyer. In His providential mind, God determined to give one Son in order to gain another son.

Jack Hayford says, "The world system will seek to reduce your view of your worth to your ability to succeed on its terms."[41] Men, if we fall for this trap, we walk right into the enemy's ploy and base our worth on a completely different standard than our Father deems appropriate. I am tempted as much as any man to find my worth in quantitative success, but while these things can be rewarding, they are at best temporal. We would all agree success is a great thing, but it is not capable of communicating to us our ultimate worth. Only the Buyer can do that.

Jesus Christ, the perfect man, offered Himself as an instrument of redemption to His Father on our behalf. He paid the price on our heads, and we were transferred from the life of Adam to the lineage of God.[42] We are no longer who we used to be. According to 2 Corinthians 5:17, we are new men because of the redemptive work of our older brother, Jesus Christ.

We are men with a new identity. We belong to God and are citizens of heaven. We know the meaning of why we are on Earth and what our purpose is for being here. And we know what we are worth. Identity, belonging, meaning, purpose, and worth—these five treasures are sought by men the world over, and they are ours, irrevocably, unequivocally, and eternally.

Given these things, are you a secure man? Absolutely! You are as secure as the Word of God. Your manhood is not open for debate, at least not with God. You can wonder about it, worry over it, discount it, demean it, debate it, and subject it to a different standard than God's, but that has as much effect on the truth of its fact as a crazy man who covers his eyes and pronounces the sun has quit shining. Do you remember Paul saying, "act like men"? It is understandable why he said that: We are men! The Father said so. It only makes sense we act like who we are.

A secure man is a man free to be himself. The doubts weakening masculinity wither themselves under the light of our Father's truth. If a man is a benchmark, a corner post for the world to strain against, gain its moral direction from, depend upon for stability, and witness God in human form, then men are equipped for this role because their security is anchored in Christ and their strength is in their Heavenly Father.

The Power of Respect

People can say all sorts of unflattering things to a man and he will find a way to deal with it. Occasionally someone will say something that stings, but most of the stuff men hear rolls off like water off a duck's back. However, if the statement has a lack of respect associated with it, men founder.

The need to be respected may well be a man's Achilles' heel. A lack of respect strikes at the core of who we are and leaves us vulnerable to people's—and the enemy's—questions regarding our masculinity. If there is a chink in a man's armor, this is it. Every man wants to be respected as a strong man, a powerful man, a man's man. He wants to be able to respect himself as a man.

We have established who we are, what we are doing, why we are doing it, whose we are, and what we are worth. Identity, meaning, purpose, belonging, and worth are the key elements of respect and self-respect. In this soil our masculine *confidence* takes root.

As a man depends upon his Heavenly Father, he has the confidence of knowing he is a strong man with the blessing of his Father, the respect of his Father, and self-respect based upon the manhood passed to him by his Father.

Brother, your Heavenly Father is proud of the man you are. He has imparted something of Himself to you, and there is nothing more rewarding for a Father. It makes Him proud to hear someone say, "He is his Father's son." Your Heavenly Father sees a likeness of Himself in you. He knows His son has become a man who will glorify Him and enjoy Him forever. In a word, this means we are secure. Secure men are confident. Secure men are stable. Secure men are honest. However, this doesn't mean secure men are impervious to hurt. It means they can accept hurt without foundering on the rocks of emotions, but just because a man is strong and secure doesn't mean his eyes will always be dry. Secure men do not bypass hurt. When pain presents itself, a secure man steps toward it.

A secure man invites people to get close to his heart. Pain is inevitable when your heart is vulnerable. Likewise, passion, joy, and peace are inevitable because these are functions of the heart. No one enjoys much who has not hurt much, and no one finds joy in suffering who is not secure.

Our Heavenly Father is the most secure person I know, and what has He done without reservation? Shared His heart. All of His hopes, dreams, plans, and visions are on the table for our response. I respect this about Him. I admire His security. More than anything, His transparency lets me know His heart is strong enough to take whatever is dished out.

You see, I am my Father's son, created in His likeness. I enjoy being around Him and am confident He enjoys the same. I am secure in Him and respected by Him. No doubt the Lord understood the inherent risks of sharing His heart with me, but determined to do so anyway in order to best connect with me. To "be like my Father" means sharing my heart, with all of the inherent risks and possibilities.

While I need to be respected as a strong man, I have no control over whether the people around me will grant me their admiration and respect. If they choose not to respect me, it will hurt, but I am secure in Christ. If they choose to respect me, together we share in the likeness of our Father.

A Man's Source

I know men; and I tell you that Jesus Christ is not a man. Superficial minds see a resemblance between Christ and the founders of empires, and the gods of other religions. That resemblance does not exist. There is between Christianity and whatever other religions the distance of infinity....

Everything in Christ astonishes me. His spirit overawes me, and his will confounds me. Between him and whoever else in the world there is no possible term of comparison. He is truly a being by himself. His ideas and his sentiments, the truth which he announces, his manner of convincing, are not explained either by human organization or by the nature of things.

The nearer I approach, the more carefully I examine everything is above me; everything remains grand—of a grandeur which overpowers. His religion is a revelation from an intelligence which certainly is not that of man. There is there a profound originality which has created a series of words and of maxims before unknown. Jesus borrowed nothing from our science. One can absolutely find nowhere, but in him alone, the imitation or the example of his life.

...I search in vain in history to find the similar to Jesus Christ, or anything which can approach the gospel. Neither history, nor humanity, nor the ages, nor nature, offer me anything with which I am able to compare it or to explain it. Here everything is extraordinary. The more I consider the gospel, the more I am assured that there is nothing there which is not beyond the march of events, and above the human mind.[43]

Such are the thoughts of Napoleon Bonaparte, the great Corsican general who commanded the armies of the French empire during her glory days, concerning Jesus Christ, your older brother. Jesus Christ is not an average man, acccording to Napolean. He is special—yet He lives in you. Your Father has commissioned Him to stick closer than a brother and you are a joint heir with Him to everything comprising your Father's household. Through His work on your behalf, you share His identity and sit with Him at your Father's right hand. This is not religious rhetoric but is characteristic of a man blessed by his Heavenly Father and accompanied by Christ.

Napoleon recognized Jesus Christ as someone extraordinary. Revelation 19:11-16 describes Him as Faithful and True, the One who wages righteous war and judgment, with eyes like flames of fire, wearing a crown indescribably magnificent, and a robe dipped in blood. He is called the Word of God, King of kings and Lord of lords, and He rides in advance of the armies of heaven. Hebrews 1:3 says, "And He is the radiance of His [God's] glory and the exact representation of His nature, and upholds all things by the word of His power. When He had made purification of sins, He sat down at the right hand of the Majesty on high." Philippians 2:10 tells us every knee in heaven and earth will bow to the name of Jesus Christ, whom John called the light and life of the world. Colossians 1:15-16 confirms that Jesus not only created all things, but is the very image of the invisible God.

He created you for Himself, and when you were lost from Him, separated by your sin and sinfulness, He sprinted across the universe to lay His life down in order to redeem you. In this way He demonstrates to men the ultimate sacrifice of manhood. As seen in those Scriptures, one of the character traits attributed to Christ is that of a warrior, honor-bound to lay His life on the line for the well-being of others. Christ, the ultimate personification of manhood, lives in you to express masculinity.

Christ alone brings the change we long to see in our lives as men. He alone can heal a wounded heart, reclaim the deficit a man feels who was never declared a man, and enable a man to portray true, masculine strength. Christ can consistently live through us the delicate balance between a warring knight and a tender redeemer. He can generate in us the medieval ideal of chivalry that combined toughness and sweetness, iron and velvet, fierceness and meekness. C.S. Lewis said it this way,

> The knight is a man of blood and iron, a man familiar with the sight of smashed faces and the ragged stumps of lopped off limbs; he is also a demure, almost maiden-like, guest in hall, a gentle, modest, unobtrusive man. He is not a compromise or happy mean between ferocity and meekness, he is fierce to the nth and meek to the nth degree.[44]

This ideal comes from Christ, whose power was expressed in weakness and whose greatest triumph was to be killed meekly. And it becomes our ideal as well—courage to serve, power to submit, greatness in humility.

Isaiah 42:13 reads, "The Lord will go forth like a warrior, He will arouse His zeal like a man of war. He will utter a shout, yes, He will raise a war cry. He will prevail against His enemies." Our Heavenly Father has not simply cooked up a bunch of nice sounding, theological concepts regarding His sons. He knows we are engaged in a battle for our hearts and lives as men. If the enemy captures us, the battle turns in his favor. God is not sitting idly by. He is Himself a warrior with blazing eyes, uttering His war cry, and He intends to prevail. The Lord intends to be our strength and source. Together we are warriors in the service of the King.

15

YOU'RE NOT JUST A MAN

"Whoa, I don't feel so hot this morning Sweetheart."

"You haven't felt good for three days, dear. Your body is run down from pushing so hard at work. Why don't you call in sick, stay home today, and catch up on your rest. I'll bet you'll feel better tomorrow."

"Umm, I appreciate your concern, but I better go on to work."

"Look, the kids won't get home until 4:00, and I'm going to be running errands most of the day. I'll put the dog outside and unplug the phone by the bed. The whole neighborhood has been sick with the flu you know, and I'd hate for you to get that. You look a little pale. I'll bet you have a temperature. Want me to get the thermometer?"

"No thanks. I can be sick at work just as easy as I can be sick at home."

"Oh! I don't understand you! You'd go to work if the world was coming to an end. You are as stubborn as a mule. You're bullheaded and obstinate. I'll bet you have the flu and will give it to everyone in the car pool. Men!"

Sound familiar? All the poor guy is doing is behaving like a man. He is a protector, a provider, a warrior. His ancestors fought with wild beasts, battled adversaries, and rode out to make war against the enemy. What if they had stayed home because they had a headache? Obstacles call for determination. Wounds heal into badges of honor. Moving forward in spite of difficulty is part of the masculine code. Staying home because of a fever feels like a duty is being shirked. Moving forward, even through hardship, is better than calling in and admitting, "I can't make it." Bly puts it like this: "He who is truly a man keeps walking dragging his guts behind."[45]

Most men resist being pushed backward and dislike distractions. We are called driven, stubborn, obstinate, inflexible, and contrary. Our heads are likened to those of bulls, pigs, and mules. Men are notorious for saying they don't understand women, but if you listen, women say the same thing about men.

Nevertheless, God wired a man to move forward. In so doing, a man is doing what men do: protecting, providing, and being a warrior. Better to deal with the enemy out there than in here. No warrior is content getting shot at without taking it to the adversary. As long as a man carries responsibility, he does what is necessary to accomplish his goal and care for those in his sphere. To do otherwise is not masculine.

The Self-Serving Man

Men who have lazy, self-indulgent flesh leave a wake of broken and wounded lives behind them because these fleshly patterns contradict everything people expect of a man. Opting for laziness is a decision to not move forward, to put off until tomorrow what should be addressed today, to jeopardize all the future holds dear for the passing pleasure of the moment. Laziness is a short-sighted, self-serving sacrifice of someone else instead of the noble self-sacrifice a man makes who is trusting

Christ. The strong man recognizes the enemy's temptation toward laziness and moves forward depending upon his Heavenly Father. To do otherwise is intolerable.

The guy who adopts a self-indulgent lifestyle places himself before those around him. If the enemy can entice a man to live in this manner, he successfully tempts him to portray the opposite of true masculinity. A man who thinks of himself before others confuses those depending upon him to protect and provide for them. This creates insecurity in everyone around him. They expect one thing and get exactly the opposite. They inherently know what they need from a man and their trust is abused. Men who succumb to these allurements from the enemy behave poorly as fathers, husbands, and friends. Rather than drawing strength from their Heavenly Father, they take advantage of His outpouring of grace in their lives. Instead of demonstrating the nobility of living for others, they portray the ignobility of living for themselves.

In addition to failing in his task as a man, the self-serving man frustrates the longing of his own heart to be masculine. This festers into deep-seated hostility, feeds the masculine doubts chasing him, and nourishes the shame bequeathed to him by Adam. Instead of basking in the glory achieved for him through the redemptive sacrifice of Jesus Christ, he fumbles the ball handed to him with his Heavenly Father's blessing.

Dear brother, if this is indicative of your lifestyle, you are living a lie. You are behaving like an immature and undisciplined boy. In addition to shirking your masculine role, you are siding with the enemy against your Father by opting for self-serving indulgence.

The prophet Ezekiel, writing in Ezekiel 36:26-27, quoted the Lord as saying, "Moreover, I will give you a new heart and put a new spirit within you; and I will remove the heart of stone from your flesh and give you a heart of flesh. And I will put My Spirit within you and cause you to walk in My statutes, and you will be careful to observe My ordinances." As a believer, the core of who you are as a man has been transformed. You are no longer the person you used to be, your heart is new and the Spirit of your Father lives in you. Act like a man. Be strong. Confess your weakness and call out to Him as your strength. Turn around and regain your bearings with your Father as your source instead of your best efforts and old ways.

Is it hard? You bet. But this is where a strong man shines. It is dangerous, too—a war, being played for keeps. But it is not hopeless. Remember who lives in you, who runs beside you, and who blessed you as a man.

The Self-Reliant Man

Without being arrogant, many men can say they are competent, dependable, and secure. They have orchestrated the construction of these great qualities into their lives, and we appreciate their confidence. After all, no one wants to go to an incompetent dentist, take his car to an undependable mechanic, or work alongside an insecure colleague. If you have committed yourself to excellence, and have pursued it with passion, understanding what really makes you a strong man will not necessarily make you a better dentist, a more capable mechanic, or a more dependable colleague. Taking inventory of your performance may not yield much of a clue about whether or not you are the kind of man your Father intends you to be.

If living a life of diligence, keeping your promises, and doing an exemplary job were indicative of a Christian man, the world would declare many pagans Christians. Just because a man bills himself as a Christian plumber doesn't mean he fixes leaks better than the plumber who is lost. If you have a water leak under your house, the lost guy who has the special tools to fix it may be the better man for the job. Many lost men behave better than many Christian men, and many unbelievers are more competent than their counterparts who are believers.

Being a godly man is more than how you conduct yourself. Your competence, dependability, and confidence are good qualities as far as responsible behavior is concerned, but if you have developed these qualities through self-determination, you might be surprised to hear your Father's comments about them. The Lord says in Romans 14:23 anything not done through faith is sin. Even good things, worthwhile things, great character qualities, and competencies not emanating from confidence in your Father's abilities are considered sinful by Him. While your performance is important to the Father, it is secondary to placing your confidence in Him. God wants you to be a strong man, but strength is discovered through dependence, not self-reliance.

In 1 Corinthians 3:10-15, Paul explains how to build our lives on the strength of the Lord:

> According to the grace of God which was given to me, as a wise master builder I laid a foundation, and another is building upon it. But let each man be careful how he builds upon it. For no man can lay a foundation other than the one which is laid, which is Jesus Christ. Now if any man builds upon the foundation with gold, silver, precious stones, wood, hay, straw, each man's work will become evident; for the day will show it, because it is to be revealed with fire; and the fire itself will test the quality of each man's work. If any man's work which he has built upon it remains, he shall receive a reward. If any man's work is burned up, he shall suffer loss; but he himself shall be saved, yet so as through fire.

First, notice Paul's encouragement. Be careful how you build on your foundation. Think about what you are doing. Manhood is not a haphazard proposition. You are not *just* a man—you are a man, a warrior, a corner post, a person of tremendous worth. You are called and commissioned by God to represent Him. It is your privilege, honor, and duty to pass the glory of manhood to the next generation.

Second, your foundation is Jesus Christ. How silly it would be to lay a solid foundation of gold, silver, and precious stones, then drive around collecting washing machine boxes to build the building. How did Christ lay the foundation? Through depending upon His Father. He was the most dependent man who ever lived—John 10:18 says the only thing Jesus did of His own initiative was lay His life down. Like our older brother, we have a choice how we will build our lives.

Third, notice that fire is going to test each man's work. Not each man—your Father has already made His determination about you. But the jury is still out regarding what you do, and the telling piece of evidence is going to be fire. You may build your life through self-reliance, or you may build your life through dependence. But only the construction built in the same manner as your older brother will withstand the flame.

Finally, notice it is the *quality* of a man's work being tested, not the quantity. It is not how much you do, but how you do it. In other words, those characteristics and acts of service produced through self-reliance, even if valuable in the eyes of the world and the church, are of a quality similar to wood, hay, and straw. On the other hand, those things produced and performed through dependence upon the resource of your Father will benefit from the testing of fire.

It is conceivable that a talented man could stand up to preach a dynamic sermon, full of Scriptural quotations and powerful points, only to see it perish into ashes because it was delivered through self-reliance. It is also possible for the same man to be convicted of his self-reliance, repent of his independent effort, and determine to drive home from church in the power of the Spirit and see that act stand the test of the fire and go down in the annals of heaven as a testimony to his Father's sufficiency.

No independent act, regardless of how beneficial or advantageous, will pass through the fire and survive a fate on the ash heap. No dependent act, regardless of how insignificant, will fail to bring glory to your Heavenly Father.

Brother, those things you consider your greatest attributes may prove to be the things the devil uses to deceive you into a lifestyle of self-reliance. When everyone around you is praising your proficiency, and the world rewards you for your competence, it is hard to realize the works of your hands are temporary and facilitate the enemy's battle plan. But it is true. Independent acts enable the enemy to accuse God of not being worthy of your confidence and dependence. Self-reliance is not indicative of a strong man.

"Trust thyself: every heart vibrates to that iron string."[46] So wrote Emerson in his essay, "Self-Reliance." Listen if you will to the plucking of that iron string. It is dull, lifeless, thudding. It is not at all like the resonance of the chord you hear when true masculinity reverberates. That is a deep, resonating, musical sound invigorating a man's heart. It is the resonance of manhood being lived out as God intended. It is the sound of a man confessing his dependence upon his Father as his source. It is the compulsion of a man's new heart dancing to the music of his Father's house.

The Example of David

Being a godly man, dependent upon your Heavenly Father, does not mean you have no opinions, cannot tap the gifts you've been given, or scrap the intellect and training you have. A strong man is dependent upon his Father and is responsible to let love guide him in all things, but that is not synonymous with passivity. A strong man capitalizes on everything afforded to him while realizing his source is the sufficiency of his Father.

Every man is intended to be a leader. Certainly not everyone is the president of a company, but every man has followers, is a leader, and should accept responsibility for leadership. It may be the only person following is your son or daughter, or the kid next door. Lead, man. Lead! They are looking to you. Demonstrate masculine strength. Show them how a strong man lives. As you exemplify true masculine strength others benefit and you are fulfilled.

Your Father wants to express Himself through you. If you fail to let this happen the world is robbed of your unique contribution of how God wants to be perceived, and the devil wins the day.

You are an integral part of what God is doing. If He establishes Himself in your life, He gains a beachhead from which to assault the enemy. Our lives are a declaration of His sufficiency and worthiness to be glorified and are exemplary of the relationship to be enjoyed with Him. We stand, therefore, as a living monument to our Father's determination to take back what is rightfully His.

First Samuel 30 is not recommended reading for children under twelve or adults with squeamish stomachs. Fire, war, plunder, slaughter, and starvation make this one chapter you don't want to put on your bedtime reading list. But it's a beautiful demonstration of how a man finds his strength in God.

David's hometown had been plundered by marauders. Everything was gone—wives, children, livestock, possessions—the city had been burned to the ground, and the men spoke of stoning David because of their bitter loss and anguished souls.

David had several options: Gather up the men ready to stone him and offer an apology, take a loyalty poll and decide whether to abdicate or fight, give up and say, "I quit," blame someone else, or put the troops in formation and march off to get even. Any of these would seem reasonable given the circumstances and distress he was feeling.

But David's reaction was extraordinary. First Samuel 30:6 reads, "David strengthened himself in the Lord his God." Calmly and methodically, David asked the Lord what He had in mind. Only then did he round up his grieving troops and pursue the scoundrel Amalekites.

Imagine David sitting alone on the rubble of what was once his home. His heart spasms with despair, longing to hear the ecstatic greeting of his family, but there is nothing but quiet. The silence is eerie. It harbors grieving men and bitter souls alone with their thoughts. Like David, they had hopes and anticipation for arriving home. They weren't expected back so soon and had been thinking how fine it would be to arrive early and see the looks of surprise. Instead, they came home to a nightmare.

David and his army gaze at a smoking valley that had once been their home. Each man labors under the weight of his own burden—except for David. He carries his own sorrow as well as the grief of every man, woman, and child under his care. Alone with the weight of the world, the fire illuminates his warrior face. No one sees his tears except God, who catches each drop.[47]

Deep inside, far into the recesses of the man, where spirit and soul become indistinguishable, David contemplates what he knows and takes issue against the enemy's counsel. *"It would be sheer folly to depend upon the resources of my army to attack this problem. The Lord doesn't need the strength of my horses or the numbers of my men. God is my refuge and strength, a very present help in trouble and in the day of my distress. I will sing of His strength and lovingkindness. My flesh and my heart may fail; but God is the strength of my heart and my portion forever. I will seek the Lord and His strength and determine to do so continually. The Lord is my strength and song. The Lord is my shield; my heart trusts Him, and I am helped; therefore my heart exults, and with my song I shall thank Him."*[48]

David does not come to the conclusion that God is still on His throne, resolve to trust Him, and begin dancing on the rubble of his burned estate. Beside the smoldering remains, alone, through tears, and while assassination plots fester in the dark, a deliberate counter-force begins taking issue with the onslaught of the enemy. With mounting determination, a spiritual tug-of-war begins. Then, ever so slowly, like a locomotive turning the wheels of a loaded freight train, the strength of the Lord begins the process of reclaiming lost ground.

Like a fighter, David doesn't bolt and run, or suppress, or sidestep the pain. He faces the challenge before him and stays in the ring. For every obstacle constructed by the enemy, David counters with confidence anchored in truth. The Bible says *all* the people were bitter and spoke of stoning him. Had I been in his sandals, my first words would have been, "OK, everybody put your rocks down and let's talk reasonably about this predicament." But David had been chased all over creation by Saul, dodged hurled spears, hid in the wilderness, and lived in caves. If asked, he would have said, "When the Lord takes me home it will be because He's ready, not because a bunch of guys decide to stone me." I don't think it ever crossed his mind to ask his men to put down their rocks.

I hear only the strength and confidence of the Lord when David says to Abiathar, "Please bring me the ephod."[49] A fearful, insecure man would not say, "Please." That simple word tells us the internal peace of God was being expressed through David. With dignity and confidence he faced the mounting hardship. He wasn't strengthened because the Lord told him he would recover all that had been lost. He was strengthened because he trusted God. David was strengthened before he ever asked for the ephod. If the people stoned him, he was strengthened. If he never saw his family again, he was strengthened. If Abiathar refused to bring him the ephod, he was strengthened. Imagine— David was strengthened even as he sat on the ashes of his burned-out home.

Being strengthened in the Lord doesn't mean your circumstances change or your emotional pain moderates. It means your confidence in the Lord surges and the Spirit begins to build spiritual momentum.

So, sit down, right where you are. Your perch may be a charred remnant, the front seat of your pickup, the kitchen table, or your mahogany and leather desk chair. Sit down and strengthen yourself in the Lord. Remind yourself, "It would be sheer folly to depend upon my resources to attack the issues before me. The gifts, power, influence, and strength available to me are a false hope for victory. God is my refuge and strength. He dwells in me in the form of the Holy Spirit and has been my stronghold and refuge when I have been distressed before. He will be the same today. My flesh and my heart may fail, but God is the strength of my heart now and throughout all time. I will seek the Lord and His strength. The Lord is my strength, my shield, and my song. I trust Him. And, just by doing so, I am helped."

You may have decisions to make, a mess to clean up, people to work with, and a few fires to put out. But as you stand up to face these issues, depend on the Lord's strength.

How Significant Is a Man?

16

Eli Yaheel Silverman rocked on the front porch, alone with his thoughts. He read some, and assisted with the administrative duties of his sizeable estate, but mostly he rocked and watched. Twice a week he walked to town for civic functions where he had obligations. On those days, he dressed for business and began his forty-five minute walk to town just after 7:00 A.M. It was only a mile and a quarter, but a man of his stature did not hurry anywhere. To do so was frowned upon. Slow and stately, leaving plenty of time to be seen approaching, talk for a few moments with the neighbors, and then leaving plenty of time to be seen departing, Eli would walk southeasterly toward his appointments. He was not particularly into making an impression, but culture dictated nobles and potentates conduct themselves in a distinguished manner. In order to not give the tongues something to wag about, and in deference to the honor he had achieved, Eli normally walked in a stately manner. But today, he sat with his thoughts.

Five years ago he had begun thinking about retirement. His sons were old enough to run things, and besides, it wasn't like he was going to drop out of sight. Counselor, financial wizard, patriarch of the family, and the one person directly responsible for sitting on the porch to make sure it didn't go anywhere, he was close at hand if needed.

But two years ago the younger son created a kink in his plans. Nathan had demanded the portion of the estate he was to inherit be liquidated and transferred to him as soon as possible. Eli couldn't believe his ears. "I beg your pardon. What did you say?" To his credit, at least he spoke sanely. Many men would have throttled the boy then and there. The son's request was more than a demand made in poor taste. In the first place, he was demanding his father jeopardize his ability to retire with the financial security he had worked to achieve for fifty years. Second, and more pointedly, the boy's demand was an implied curse. In effect, the son was saying, "I wish you were dead, Dad. But since you are not, I'll live like you are dead by taking my inheritance now. Liquidate, please."

Eli converted to cash that portion of his holdings stipulated in the will for his younger son, and at a family dinner in his son's honor gave him his inheritance. Before the meal was over, Eli blessed his son, toasted him with the finest wine in the house, and gave him a twelve-inch decorative dagger to wear on his belt as a gift. It would be symbolic to everyone of the status of the home from which he came.

That night at the party was the last time Eli saw his younger son. Nathan either left late in the evening or early the next morning. Either way, the boy was gone and hadn't bothered to say good-bye. And Eli wondered if he had done the right thing, been too hard, too soft, too giving, or not giving enough.

He was a pragmatic man who knew regret was like a cold supper. Second-guessing himself would serve no purpose. Even though his questions were buried below the surface of his consciousness, he controlled his mind. The real issue occupying his thoughts as he sat on the porch was his son. Though no longer a boy, Nathan was still his son, and Eli loved him beyond words.

He had let him go, but he still watched the road in case the boy returned.

Eli built the rambling home and estate headquarters on the highest hill in the south section. If there was a breeze, Eli felt it, and if there were mosquitoes in the evening, they stayed down the hill. From the front gate to the house was three blocks, close enough Eli could recognize passersby but far enough away to preserve the solitude of the Silverman estate. There were orchards on the west side of the lane and vineyards on the east. Hired men tended both sides of the road, managed by foremen, who were managed by the superintendents, who were managed by Joab, Eli's eldest son.

Joab was a diligent man with a natural affinity for business affairs. He was a hands-on boss who managed by example, something he had seen Eli model for thirty years. His capability gave Eli confidence regarding the future of the estate. In many ways, Eli knew Joab had more natural talent for running the business than he had. Working together, the two of them had rebuilt their working capital after Nathan left. Only now, two years later, was there any assurance their plan would work. Solid business practice, a few calculated risks, hard work, and much prayer had averted a major catastrophe. Time would only travel so fast, and it was the key to the success of their comprehensive, ten-year plan. To believe the family would ever be the same after suffering such a loss would be naïve. To believe the estate would survive and regain its market dominance was the hope Eli and Joab shared.

The afternoon briefing by the superintendents went well. The crops were looking good and the plant yield appeared to be five to seven percent higher than their more optimistic projections. They attributed the favorable outlook to more cultivation around the plants, and yes, the income from the increased yield would more than offset the increased labor costs to do the cultivation. But that meant more time in the field for Joab and more time reviewing labor reports for Eli—a necessary price to pay, but one well worth the benefits.

Eli worked best early in the morning and rocked best in the late afternoon. While he knew most everyone in town, there were migrant workers and an occasional visitor to the area whom he didn't recognize as they walked past his property on the county road. Given all he was thinking about, Eli's mind didn't interrupt him with the notice of a stranger passing by his gate, and at first glance the distant figure was just another traveler on the road. But this was no ordinary traveler.

The man paused for a long time at the gate leading into the Silverman estate. While unusual, this was not extraordinary. Folks often slowed down to look up Eli Silverman's road, at the sprawling vineyards and expansive orchards framing the manor house. Even though Eli Yaheel Silverman did not think of himself as a man with a famous reputation, it was nevertheless the truth, and gawkers often went out of their way just to pass the renowned gates and look up the road. They didn't often stop and linger, as this fellow was doing. But no matter—looks are free.

Eli's mind arrested his detached thought, drawing his attention to the familiar in what he at first thought was strange. The traveler at his gate was now walking up the road toward the house, and that is precisely what captured Eli's notice. No, not that the stranger was on his property, but that his walk was not strange. Eli knew this man's walk, and he knew this was no stranger. It was Nathan!

There was no thought given to his actions. No sound. No wave. No whistle. Upon impulse, with love compelling him, Eli bolted from his rocker, grabbed the hem of his robe, and kicked off his sandals all in one motion, leaping off the porch. Without thought of his dignity or the esteem afforded him in society, Eli ran down the road toward his approaching son, straightening out the curves in the road as he went.

While Eli recognized Nathan, Nathan was unsure the man running toward him was his father. It looked like his dad, but men of his age and notoriety didn't run anywhere, not to mention hiking their robes up and kicking off their shoes. The father almost knocked Nathan off balance grabbing him. Although the stench was almost unbearable, Eli wrapped his arms around Nathan's disheveled body and buried his face against his son's neck.

Nathan began his hoarse, groveling, rehearsed speech of self-deprecation, detailing his failure and conveying his contrition. Eli heard, but only acknowledged with the arm around his son's shoulder. In typical fatherly fashion, he interrupted Nathan's speech mid-sentence to speak as the patriarch of the Silverman family. Motioning to slaves, hired hands, managers, and a super-intendent or two, he ordered a new robe and a new pair of shoes be brought immediately. "Bring a Silverman signature ring and put it on his hand," he added, "and forget the chicken casserole for dinner. We are having steak tonight, and everyone is invited to the party! Nathan, my son, is home!"

The implications of Eli's statement were clear. Work priorities had just been altered. Runners were sent to the other sections of the farm. Hoes and rakes were put down and musical instru-ments picked up. The cooks were to be assisted, previous engagements were postponed, and the main hall was to be re-arranged with the furniture pushed back against the wall so the floor was clear for dancing. Nothing was to deter the celebration of Nathan's homecoming.

Once Eli was certain Nathan was being cared for properly, he walked through the kitchen and out the back door toward the north field where Joab and a crew of men were working. The run-ner had delivered his message and the crew was returning to clean up, but they were not coming in characteristic fashion. The men lagged behind Joab. Ordinarily, they would have been bunched up in a pack, tired, but laughing and enjoying the camaraderie among men who have worked shoulder-to-shoulder to accomplish the day's work. Joab walked resolutely, twenty paces in front of a somber crew who appeared beaten. Eli quickened his pace.

The crew split off the road and crossed the pasture toward the bunk houses in order to afford Joab and Eli privacy as they met. Joab dropped his implements and launched into his speech. Like Nathan's, it was rehearsed, but it did not contain the humility of his younger brother's. Joab's speech was conceived in anger and indignation and delivered with all of the offense festering for two years since his little brother had bailed out and left them in the lurch. Eli listened. He did not interrupt Joab as he had Nathan. He did not reach out to touch his elder son as he had his younger. He understood perfectly what Joab was trying to say. Eli knew the intent before Joab ever concocted the words in his mind…and it broke his heart. Eli's fears were confirmed.

Nathan had demanded what was his, taken it selfishly, squandered it thoughtlessly, embarrassed himself, and dragged the Silverman reputation into bed with prostitutes, into drunken orgies, through the gutters of human degradation, and finally into the pig pens of destitution and desperation. The only inkling of his heritage with which he returned home was the dagger Eli had blessed him with before he left, and this he was willing to renounce if Eli would allow him to return to the estate and live near him as a hired slave.

Joab never understood who he was. He worked for his father trying to *earn* the inheritance that was his by birth. In so doing, he discounted every effort his father made to share his heritage with him. He performed admirably, used his talents to recapitalize the business, built loyalty among the men he oversaw, and competently conceived a plan to restore dignity to the Silverman name, but he did so without understanding his true role. For all of the time spent with his father, Joab still worked to earn his place, never comprehending his dad had bequeathed that place to him the moment he was born. All of the outward symbolism that indicated

Joab was heir to everything called Silverman couldn't convince Joab in his heart he was Joab Silverman, Eli's eldest son, and not simply general manager of the estate.

Just as Eli had surmised, Nathan had returned from a far country where he had run chasing after an identity he already possessed. But Joab was still in a far country trying to earn the identity he already possessed. One son, Nathan, was in the house celebrating his realization, the other, Joab, was standing outside the house, nursing resentment, and complaining he never received what he was due. Eli understood what Joab had yet to discover: The far country can be just off the porch where the father rocks and watches.

Time and time again Eli had said to Joab, "Son, everything I have is yours." With that statement he was hoping to convince Joab of the one simple fact he had been trying to communicate for thirty years: He was a son. With that one statement Eli was trying to communicate to Joab that Nathan was the beneficiary of a celebration thrown by his father while he was the beneficiary of his father's abiding joy.

Eli bent down, picked up the implements Joab had thrown into the dirt, and handed them to him, patted his son on the shoulder, and returned to the house. The party would not last long. Tomorrow was a work day, Nathan was too weak to stay up late, and the evening shadows were already getting long.

After the celebration died down and the house had grown quiet, Eli padded softly across the tile foyer in his bare feet to the front door, pulled it open, and stepped onto the front porch. The south breeze brought the smells he was familiar with of ripening fruit in the orchards and vineyards, and dew settling the dust of the day. A bird called from his perch near the front gate and reminded Eli of Nathan's tentative entrance only hours before. He smiled and scratched the back of his neck. His son who was lost had been found and was now asleep upstairs.

The father eased across the long porch to his chair, sat down, pushed against the planks under his feet, and began rocking. Once again his thoughts carried him off the porch into a far country, listening, searching, running, and ever watching for his son to return.

The Father's Heart

The story of the prodigal son, which Jesus told in Luke 15, should actually be called the story of the prodigal sons, because both boys were in the far country. It is irrelevant that one acted like he was in the far country and the other did not. The point is that the far country doesn't have to be a long way away. The theme of this story is not Nathan, even though those of us who have grown up in the church have heard umpteen sermons about him. Nor is the primary theme the older son, Joab. The central theme of this story is about the father who watches, who runs to meet his youngest son, who goes out to search for his eldest son, and who will not rest until they are both home.[50] It is a story about a father determined to give everything that is his to his sons. The behavior of the father tells us the significance of a man.

How would you have responded if you were Eli Silverman? If I was on the porch I probably would have stood up, but I would not have run down the lane to meet Nathan. My pride would have kept me on the porch, my sense of fairness, my irritation with having to change plans because of what he had done, my dignity and reputation, my honor. With that attitude, I'm struck by the realization that I align myself more with the scribes and Pharisees grumbling at Jesus because he ate with sinners, thus prompting the telling of this story in the first place. That revelation does not even afford me the luxury of identifying with the young son who acted so sinfully, let alone with Eli.

If you were God—the heavenly Father—how would you respond when a prodigal began his trek up the road toward home? He did not respond like we might. As soon as we made our first step toward home, disregarding who He is and the dignity afforded Him, He caught His regal robes by the hem, kicked off His sandals, leaped off of the porch of heaven, and bolted down the lane to fall on our neck and declare that a celebration should begin because the son whom He had lost was found.

And which son do you identify with in this story, Nathan or Joab? Much to my chagrin, I see more of myself in Joab. I have lived much of my life like a hired man trying to earn God's inheritance, not understanding His celebration when a prodigal comes home. I have believed the status I enjoy is my just due for working and being responsible. I have confused my Father's blessing with the belief that I can earn His favor. And the thing most startling about this story is that it is Nathan who returns home and Joab who remains distant. Did he come in and participate in the celebration for his brother? Did he come to his senses and join his father on the front porch later in the evening? Did he realize the distinction between himself and the hired men who worked for him? Or did he stomp up the back staircase to his room, go to bed early, and head out early the next morning for work? The story doesn't say. That ending is yet to be written. But one thing is certain: The father sits on the porch and watches, waiting for him to make his first step toward home.

There is no question about which of the two sons was the most responsible—it was certainly Joab. But there is also no question about which son was farthest from home. That too was Joab. Through commitment and hard work, Joab produced what the Silverman estate needed. But this story is not about competent business administration. It is about the motive driving the man. If we could interview Eli he would tell us how invaluable Joab's contribution was to the success of the business, but he would be quick to say his connection with Joab had little to do with the business and everything to do with being his father. Eli was connected to Joab because he was family. Yet, Joab was connected to Eli because he believed he had earned his place, especially in light of Nathan's irresponsibility.

As strange as it may seem, Nathan knew who he was and Joab did not. While he shared his father's name, Joab was working to earn his recognition. Nathan knew his father loved him, but Joab was trying to earn Eli's love through his competence and responsible behavior. Nathan realized his behavior betrayed his identity, while Joab believed his job described his identity. Nathan knew his significance emanated from who he was, and Joab believed his significance was derived from what he did. Nathan's return signaled he wanted to be close to his father. The question left unanswered is whether Joab returned from the far country where he was working to establish his identity apart from his father.

The Curse of the Capable

How easy it is for those blessed with capability, talent, and initiative to base their identity on achievements and accolades. In so doing, it becomes difficult to return from the far country. Our Heavenly Father values the work of our hands, but He is interested in the motive driving what we do. He appeals to us as sons, longs for a connection between His heart and ours, and blesses us because we are His, not because of what we do for Him. Herein lies the great secret to a man's significance. Joab and Nathan were significant because they were loved by their father. The same is true for you and me.

Jesus Christ knew who He was, and that He was loved by His Father. You can know both of these things as well. Your significance must be anchored in your identification with your Father. This is the footing, the cement mix at the base of the corner post.

An evaluation of Nathan's fleshly patterns yields a declaration of worthlessness. Try as he might, even after the expenditure of a sizeable fortune, Nathan's best efforts were unproductive. It does not take much imagination to come up with a list of Nathan's sins while he was in the far country. On the other hand, we have to conclude that Joab's best efforts were productive. Through his own genius he developed a working plan, developed a team of employees that honored him, and revitalized the family business. If the superintendents of the Silverman estate were asked who to attribute the success of the economic recovery to, they would say without hesitation Joab Silverman. Listing Joab's sins is a difficult proposition. While no one in his right mind would want to repeat Nathan's history, the line of those hoping to emulate Joab's successes would be long.

Yet, the Scripture is clear: God hates sin, and anything not originating from faith—that is, confidence in God and His abilities—is sin. Nathan and Joab were both in the far country.

The flesh is not capable of defining our true identity for us or establishing that we are loved by our Father. If asked about this, Nathan would readily agree, and as the story indicates, we are left with Joab still mulling this over in his mind.

Nathan, Joab, your Father has run to meet you. He has called you by His own name and bequeathed His unequivocal, irrevocable blessing upon you. He has filled you with His Spirit, promised to be your strength, and said He is your source. There is no need for you to walk after your old ways. Every time you opt for the devil's temptation to walk after your flesh, you depart from home for the far country. Your significance is not in the far country. It is in your Father's love.

THE WAR STRATEGY FROM HELL

17

The radio cackled its familiar musical chimes signifying the news was up next. There was the station identifier, introduction of the radio personalities, the traffic report, and then the voice of the President of the United States, Lyndon Baines Johnson, delivering something similar to a weekly radio address. Speaking in his trademark Texas drawl, LBJ spoke incisively about current events in the late 1990s—even though he died in 1973. At first I thought this was a stroll down memory lane, but it turned out to be some sort of hoax. At first I was taken in by the voice. Whoever the impersonator was, he was excellent. But the deception became apparent when "the President" began his discussion of current events.

I enjoy a good impersonator mimicking famous people. But not being famous myself, I had never given much thought to what it would be like to have someone impersonate me. However, this is exactly what the devil does. Just like the guy on the radio, Satan impersonates a dead man and discusses current events in an attempt to deceive me, the listener, into thinking it really is the dead man talking.

The Scriptures teach that the old me—who I was in Adam—was crucified with Christ and no longer lives.[51] The part of me that loved to sin and rebel against God is no longer alive. If I am going to sin, I must be tempted to do so and agree with the devil that the temptation is a good idea. Since my old, sin-loving nature is no longer alive, I won't come up with rebellious, sinful thoughts on my own. That's the devil's job.

In an effort to accomplish his task and entice me to sin, the devil has devised an insidious but profoundly simple method of temptation: He makes his offer disguised as the old, dead, sinful man, and correlates his suggestion with my unique version of living independent of God. This pattern of independence is what the Bible calls "flesh"—the patterns I have developed for living life. Just like the guy on the radio impersonating LBJ, the devil impersonates the man who was crucified with Christ—my old, sinful self—and makes his temptation match my version of the flesh.

Like any good impersonator, he suggests his temptation using first person, singular pronouns—I, me, my, mine. He speaks using my tone of voice and regional accent. Said another way, the devil disguises himself as me and offers thoughts that seem like my own ideas, addressing life as I am used to doing in the flesh.[52] His angle is to try to deceive me into thinking it is my idea to rebel against my Father and that is a lie originating from the inner sanctum of hell. Sinning is not my idea or desire. Satan is verbalizing his own thoughts and values, not mine. At the core of my new heart, I do not want to rebel against my Father. I do not want to walk after the flesh. As a new man in Christ, a son of the Most High God, my Father, I have been set free from having no choice about whether to sin or not. I do not have to go along with Satan's offerings.[53]

But the enemy's punch is always a one-two punch. Before you know what hit you the first time, he lands his second lick. He accuses you with second person, singular pronouns—you, your, yours. All the while he hides behind his cowardly disguise of using your voice.

So the devil offers you a temptation correlated with your old program (flesh), accuses you with it, and then condemns you for the sorry thoughts you are generating. And as you have probably gathered by now, his condemnation—just like his temptation—is delivered disguised as you. With the appropriate first person pronouns, he condemns the new man for a treasonously sinful thought that wasn't yours to begin with. It is a right jab, a left to the body, and then a right to the jaw from an enemy in disguise.

Of course, if all you're doing is listening to that voice of Satan, you haven't sinned yet. You are not responsible until you adopt the enemy's temptation as your prescribed plan of action. Once you have endorsed his idea, you are culpable. Until that time, you are simply being tempted, and Jesus was tempted the Bible tells us. It is not a sin to be enticed by the devil. Furthermore, as long as you are engaged in the battle of this life, you will never escape temptation. The enemy will assault you during your Bible study, your prayer time, the ball game, while you are at dinner, and during church. Name the place, and he will attack.

Satan will tempt you to return to your old plan to gain significance because he is intent on enticing you to live independently, and in so doing discredit your Father. As you find yourself embroiled in his onslaught, walking after the flesh will seem like a legitimate option. It feels normal, and it may even seem productive. Such is the nature of this war.

In the thick of the battle, there are times when I make poor choices, go along with the devil's suggestions, and behave contrary to my heart and true identity. In other words, I sin. I act like Nathan and Joab, behaving like someone I am not. When I buy into Lucifer's lie, I have a responsibility to acknowledge my sin and turn my face toward home, embracing the forgiveness provided by my Father's grace.

A Coward's Fight

There is nothing more disarming than the way a coward fights. One summer during high school I was tapped to start in place of another guy on a church softball team. As you would imagine, the guy I was replacing was ticked. Just before we began warming up, he filled the inside of my cleats with mud, and then while I was cleaning my shoes out, he came up behind me and hit me in the ribs with his fist and forearm, cracking two of my ribs and knocking the breath out of me. I was too busy trying to regain my ability to breathe to get in on the team fight, but the other guys nearly killed him. Determined to not let him get the best of me, I went ahead and played in the game.

This altercation is indicative of the way a coward fights. He strikes from behind, kicks you when you are down, throws low blows, will bite and scratch if given the opportunity, and avoids the real issue of his insecurity at all costs.

You are engaged in a spiritual war being waged by the antithesis of God. He is a hate-filled, avaricious coward who is fighting for his life. Do you not think he is aware of the fact God has prepared hell for him and his demons?[54] If he is unsuccessful in his bid for God's throne, there is no doubt in his mind where he is going to spend eternity. His fight is an ignoble, desperate act of self-preservation and vacuous pride.

You must fight against him with spiritual weapons,[55] respond to him with truth, and set your mind on what your Father says about you. How you feel, the track record of successes afforded you by your productive flesh, or what the enemy is recommending will lead you down the wrong road, diverging from the road toward home. Say no to the enemy's deception.[56] Set your mind on what true strength is, who your source is, and how your significance is actually determined.[57]

Act like a man. As you do so, you will seize victory and avert defeat, procuring for yourself the confidence of a man who is strong, secure, and significant. To do otherwise is to engage the enemy on his terms and reduce yourself to joining a coward's fight. Not only is this not a winnable fight, there is no honor or masculine strength in such a battle. Cowards fight to preserve their insecurities. A man knows he is strong, secure, and significant. From this basis he wages a noble battle and continues forward on the road to victory.

A MAN'S SECURITY

18

The three men were up early and left by the south trail. Climbing is difficult anytime, but especially so in the dark. Nevertheless, Moses, Aaron, and Hur eased up the hill under the cover of darkness, moving toward the purple-black sky soon to be tinged with the lavender and pink of a desert sunrise. The coarse, desert plants pulled at their woven clothing and the sandstone rocks snagged the toes of their sandals.

Below them the Israelite camp rustled with eager, anxious, and fearful men anticipating a military advance against the Amalekites. Since leaving Egypt, the Israelites' concerns have been for life's essentials: food, water, and shelter. They are not warriors. As if surviving in this harsh land were not challenge enough, the Amalekites have been attacking the stragglers bringing up the rear of the Israelite parade to the promised land. Losses are inevitable when marching a million or more people through the arid expanses of the Sinai, but these losses are especially hard to take. Why didn't the cowards attack face-to-face and fight like men are supposed to fight? Why prey upon the weak, infirmed, and elderly? Moses, the leader of Israel, made his decision. No more of these losses. Israel will fight.

Combat is confusing, even to the seasoned soldier. Perhaps that is why Moses' instructions to Joshua were simple. Israel was a non-warring people who did not know how to draft a sophisticated battle plan. "Joshua, choose men for us, and go out, fight against Amalek. Tomorrow I will station myself on the top of the hill with the staff of God in my hand." Thus ended the briefing. Joshua's orders and Moses' intentions were clear—they would fight Amalek at Rephidim in the morning.

This was the first opposition Israel met as they left Egypt and made their way toward the land God promised them. The Amalekites were not God-fearing people and had an ancestral hatred for Israel. Amalek, the tribe's namesake, was Esau's grandson. Esau was the twin brother of Jacob, whom God would later call Israel. While Esau was the older of the two boys and heir to his father's blessing, he traded his birthright to Jacob for a bowl of stew. Though it didn't seem like a big deal at the time, this event haunted Esau for the rest of his life, creating hatred between himself and his brother. Now this hated man's ancestors—the Amalekites—were ambushing his brother's ancestors in the wilderness.

Esau and Jacob were the sons of Isaac, the miracle child born to Abraham and Sarah. His birth was the fulfillment of God's promise to Abraham that he would be the father of a great nation. Indeed he was, for Moses was leading several million Israelites toward the land God set aside for them. But first they had to deal with Esau's descendents.

On one side of the battlefield, Amalek began to stir. Campfires flickered in the valley as Moses, Aaron, and Hur climbed through the dark toward the sunrise and a day of warfare. Every man, whether on the battlefield or the mountain above, thought the thoughts all men think before going to war. Each fought himself first in order to master his fears and advance against the enemy.

Dawn revealed battle lines forming. The wilderness was still, but with the wave of Joshua's hand, the silence was punctured and two age-old enemies careered toward each other across the dirt skin of the wilderness.

The battle quickly descended into brutal hand-to-hand combat. Neither nation had an arsenal filled with the weapons of warfare, so they beat one another with sticks and rocks and slings. They grappled with their hands and teeth and feet. From Moses' place on the hill, the ebb and flow of men fighting for their lives and the cause inspiring their courage is evident. But even more apparent than the horror of mortal combat is that Israel prevails only while Moses holds his hand up clutching the rod of God. When he drops his arms to rest, Amalek surges forward and Israelites litter the battlefield with their suffering and death.

What is at stake is no mystery, and what needs to be done is clear: Moses must not drop his hands and lower the rod of God. Aaron and Hur plunge into action. They carry a large stone and position it so that Moses can sit on the rock and view the progress of the battle. Aaron steps to Moses' right side and Hur to his left. From here they cradle his arms in the crook between their forearm and biceps and Moses' hands are steadied.

As the sun melts into the desert horizon, Amalek is overrun by Joshua and the Israelites. Wild cheers rise from the valley floor in concert with the cheers echoing from the hilltop vantage point. Israel has won the day and Amalek is repulsed.[58]

I Read Your Book

It is said that as General George Patton watched his armored divisions defeat the brilliant German commander Irwin Rommel in the desert of North Africa during World War II, he screamed across the desert from his hilltop vantage point toward the fleeing Rommel, "I read your book!" The implication is clear: Patton knew Rommel's tactics and gained an advantage over him because he read his stories.

The story of Israel's battle against Amalek at Rephidim is significant. After all, thousands of men died and drained their blood into the battlefields striving to possess an ignominious piece of real estate. What does this story tell us about our enemy that will give us the advantage in our war against evil? While this was their first battle, Israelite history is replete with many battles and great war stories. Why is this one in particular important? What made Amalek, the descendant of Esau, such an insidious enemy? Major Ian Thomas writes,

> What was the birthright that Esau despised? The birthright was the promise that God had given to Abraham that in his seed all the families of the earth should be blessed. That is to say, the birthright involved the birth of Christ, the One who would redeem man from his lost condition, and restore him to his true relationship to God, making him dependent once more upon the One whose presence is life, and who alone can enable man to behave as man, as God intended man to be.

> This was the birthright—that God was prepared in the person of His incarnate Son, to make man man again, and to restore him to his true humanity—and Esau despised the birthright! Esau said in his heart, "Sunday school talk! I don't need this kind of kid's stuff! I have all that it takes to be man, apart from God!" There was perpetuated in him the basic lie perpetrated by Satan in Adam—"You are what you are, by virtue of what you are, and not by virtue of what God is. You can lose God and lose nothing."[59]

If that attitude is not a picture of the flesh, I don't know what is. Esau's despise for his birthright is the same independence from which our fleshly patterns are constructed. It leaves us vulnerable to the devil's temptation to opt for the flesh instead of living according to our birthright as sons of God.

The Major goes on to say, "Amalek is a picture of the flesh, seeking at all costs to bar the onward journey of God's redeemed people."[60] As Galatians 5:17 puts it, "The flesh sets its desire against the Spirit, and the Spirit against the flesh; for these are in opposition to one another." Satan will attempt to use our fleshly patterns to misdirect us from the moment we turn toward home.

When Exodus 17:13 says Joshua "overwhelmed" Amalek, it is literally saying he weakened Amalek. Israel would encounter this foe time and time again as they tried to follow the Lord. In Judges 3, we are told Amalek was allied with the king of Moab against Israel and kept her in slavery for eighteen years. Amalek was the downfall of Israel's first king, Saul, who was instructed by the prophet Samuel to utterly destroy everything having to do with Amalek. Saul did not, and it cost him his kingdom and Israel her peace.[61] The warring crowd that razed David's home town to rubble in 1 Samuel 30 was from Amalek. Given the fact we war against the flesh, can we escape the importance of dealing decisively with our flesh and resisting the enemy by walking in the Spirit? Will we learn from Israel's battles and determine to make no provision for the flesh?

Amalek began a cowardly, rear assault upon the weak and straggling as soon as Israel was free from bondage in Egypt. The enemy will assault you via your fleshly vulnerabilities and weaknesses as soon as you align yourself with your Heavenly Father. As long as Moses held up the rod of God, Joshua prevailed over Amalek, but as soon as he dropped his arms, the enemy advanced. In a similar way, we cannot diminish the imperative of lifting our Father up to the place of preeminence in our lives and hope to dominate against the enemy. If we focus our eyes on our own resources and attempt to live life via self-effort, the enemy will capitalize on our flesh to assault the kingdom of God and cost us our peace. Considering what is at stake, should we propose to climb to the top of the hill, oversee the battle, and hope to lift Christ up by ourselves?

A man's security is in Christ and with other men. A secure man knows who he is, that he is loved by his Father, and that he is not alone—three tenets of masculinity the enemy of God is intent on undermining.

Never Climb Alone

Paul states in Galatians 5:16, "But I say, walk by the Spirit, and you will not carry out the desire of the flesh." In the original Greek this verse literally reads, "Walk by the Spirit, and you will not, by no means, carry out the desires of the flesh." While using a double negative is poor English grammar, it provides great theological insight into the power that is ours in Christ through His indwelling Spirit.

A strong man is a man who has discovered how to depend upon his Father. A man anchored in Christ is a man anchored as a corner post. It is no accident Moses sat upon a rock as he oversaw Israel's battle against Amalek. Throughout the Bible, God is a rock[62] and Jesus is called the rock in the wilderness who provided spiritual life (1 Corinthians 10:4). Just as Moses positioned himself on the rock and lifted up the rod of God to have victory over Amalek, we must position ourselves in Jesus Christ, the rock, and lift up our hands to our Heavenly Father as a sign of dependence on Him if we are to experience victory over our Amalek—the flesh.

Moses positioned himself on the rock and lifted up the rod of God's power. He exemplified a holy, Spirit-led determination to depend upon God for deliverance from Amalek, who was deterring Israel from the promise of God. But notice Moses did not go to the hill above the battle by himself. He took Aaron and Hur with him. These two men brought the stone Moses sat upon, and they stood on either side of him and supported his hands while the battle raged. When Moses tired and let his guard down, Amalek began to make advances. It was then these two trusted advisers steadied his hands and helped him be strong.

No one but you can decide to wrap your arms around the blessing of your Father and embrace it. And no one can anchor you in Christ unless you first determine to side with Him. Like Moses, you must make a determined, Spirit-led choice to climb the hill above the battle and station yourself. But a wise man, a strong man, a man who knows and understands the significance his Father has placed upon him, will not climb the hill without a companion. Dr. Howard Hendricks, professor emeritus at Dallas Theological Seminary, says, "A man who is not in a group with other men is an accident waiting to happen."[63]

If it had not been for Aaron and Hur on that fateful day in Exodus 17, where would Israel be? How would the battle against Amalek have ended? I wonder if Joshua would have lived through the battle to lead Israel across the Jordan River and into the promised land. If it had not been for Aaron and Hur, would Moses have been innovative enough to think of a way to keep his hands raised by himself?

We can speculate about these questions, but we don't have to answer them because Aaron and Hur were there. And Exodus says Moses' hands were steady because of them. He conducted himself with fidelity because Aaron was on one side and Hur on the other.

The result was that Amalek was weakened. Israel moved forward toward the promise of God. The stragglers made the trip instead of dying at the hands of Amalek in the wilderness. Because one man took two trusted buddies with him to the hill above the battle, positioned himself on the rock, depended upon God, and relied upon his friends to support him, Israel had victory over the flesh. A man knows his security is in Christ and with other men.

The Fence Row

When Cecil and I began building fence, we started by setting the corner posts and tying them together with two-by-sixes. This is a portrait of what happened with Moses, Aaron, and Hur during the battle at Rephidim. Moses was seated securely on a rock with his arms held out straight from his body, parallel to the ground, and at a ninety-degree angle. Seated on rocks beside him were Aaron and Hur. Their hands grasped Moses' arms just below his shoulders, so that his hands and arms rested on their shoulders. Do you see the corner post configuration? All three men were anchored in rock. They were secure. Their arms were like two-by-six ties binding them together for stability.

During men's conferences I often ask three men from the audience to join me on the platform. Using each man as a living post, I construct a corner post configuration and have their inter-locked, outstretched arms simulate the cross members between the posts. Quite often this visual of three men, linked together, supporting each other, their feet firmly anchored in Christ, com-municates volumes and the audience breaks into applause. Men are able to envision the strength and support they can have.

Dear brother, you are anchored in Christ, secure in Him. He has been commissioned by our Father to take up residence in you, to run the race with you, to take you and make you part of His life. In Him, you are significant. In Him, you stand as a corner post. In Him you are strong.

You and He are engaged in a great war to determine which spiritual power will rule in the hearts and lives of people. The enemy is relentless with guerilla warfare tactics, attacking from the rear, knocking off the unsuspecting, capitalizing on the undis-ciplined, taking advantage of the weak and wounded. He assaults equally as well from the front, brashly accusing God of being unworthy, demeaning the name of Christ, and casting aspersion on the power of the Holy Spirit. Hiding behind the defenses of societal opinions, advancing through craters in the moral ground, firing missiles at our flesh, and touting isolation among men as philosophical truth, the devil and his angels wage war against

God and against men to gain the high ground. Satan pokes at the credibility of God and tries to panic you and me.

But you are anchored. You know who wins the war. Now decide who will win this battle. Climb the hill, brother, but *take someone with you*. Trusted men. Faithful friends. Colleagues who will watch your backside. Dependable brothers who will position themselves in Christ beside you, lock arms with you, and stand by you shoulder-to-shoulder until the day is done and the victory won.

Men are warriors and warriors fight battles. Battles cost lives, but men lay their lives down for a cause greater than themselves so those they love can experience life in all its fullness. A secure man does not wince at laying his life down for a great cause, because he knows who he is and where he is going. He is a redeemer, protector, and provider. He is a man loved by his Father and seated with his elder brother at his Father's right hand. He is a knight, bound by the honor of his Father's blessing. Still, no warrior wants to fight alone. As Stu Weber says,

> Down deep at the core, every man needs a man friend. Down deep at the core, every man needs a brother to lock arms with. Down deep at the core, every man needs a soul mate. Yes, beyond question, our wives are to be our most intimate companions. We're to be willing to die for our wives and our children instantly, and many of us are ready to do just that. But within the willingness to die for family and home, something inside us longs for someone to die *with*...someone to die *beside*...someone to lock step with. Another man with a heart like our own.[64]

John Wayne fought alone in *True Grit*. Clint Eastwood rode alone in *Pale Rider*. Alan Ladd went to town by himself in *Shane* to settle the score against the bad guys. Elijah took on the 450 prophets of Baal by himself on Mount Carmel, and Jesus went alone into the wilderness to be tempted by the devil. There are times when men stand alone, and we are inspired by their great stories of heroism…but these are exceptions to the rule.

Comrades in Arms

Strength is not isolation. Men were never created to be loners. In fact, the first thing God says about men in the Bible is that it is not good for them to be alone. This does not necessarily mean every man should be married, but that men are not meant solely for isolation.

Men need men. On the night of His betrayal, Jesus asked His three closest friends to pray and keep watch with Him.[65] If you will recall, Pete, Jim, and John all fell asleep while Jesus was experiencing the deepest grief of His life. On three occasions He woke them up and pleaded with them to watch and pray with Him. We often think about the lessons the disciples must have learned about prayer and vigilance from this experience, and try to make application to our own lives, but we rarely consider what Jesus' motive was for asking his three buddies to go with Him deeper into the garden. While He was fully divine, Jesus was also fully human. His needs as a man were no different than our needs. He called out repeatedly to Peter, James, and John because *He needed to know His friends were standing with Him,* praying beside Him, looking out for Him, struggling with Him against the evil one, fighting for Him, and laying their lives down in intercession on His behalf. Christ wanted to know if there was anyone close enough to die with Him in the event it came to that.

Think of it—God in human form calling out for His friends in a time of need. God, whose creative genius stipulated no sparrow should lack a friend with whom to roam, chased all the way across the universe to a dark garden outside Jerusalem and called three times for his friends. God became a man and needed men enough to lay His life down for the cause He believed in.

Jesus, the consummate warrior, called for a man to stand beside Him during His final battle.

Men need the friendship of other men. Proverbs 27:17 says, "Iron sharpens iron, so one man sharpens another." I believe our Father, in His infinite wisdom, knew we would understand our intangible relationship with Him better if we could experience a tangible friendship with other men. From these relationships, God infers what our relationship with Him is like. Men need men because it enables our Father to offer a meaningful parallel, as though He were saying, "Pres, My relationship with you is like the friendship you have with your friend, Cecil." While we are to be dependent upon our Heavenly Father, He has provided other men to help us see how a dependent man behaves.

A lone man is scary. Men are pack animals, just like wolves. A lone wolf, as they are called, is an animal not bonded to a pack. Quite often it is these animals that become desperate for survival, become dangerous, and have to be destroyed because they do not have the survival advantage of the pack. It is these animals that die alone.

The alpha male, or leader of the wolf pack, is a team player that has earned the respect, admiration, and loyalty of the pack. I read a story recently about an alpha male wolf seriously injured during an attack on a musk ox. He dragged himself under a balsam fir and lay there awaiting his fate. I expected to read about an ensuing power struggle for pack dominance and how the injured wolf was never heard from again. On the contrary, the wolf who was heir apparent to pack leadership coordinated the pack's hunting and safety during the alpha male's absence and carried food to the injured wolf until he recovered and assumed command of the pack again. Men, we are pack animals and are to be like that.

I visited a man several years ago who moved from Fort Worth to Philadelphia. As he and I were eating a slice of pizza together and getting caught up on life, he told me he felt isolated.

His church was a forty-five minute train and bus ride away, his colleagues at work had markedly different values than he did, and he hadn't really connected with anyone in his neighborhood. That man recognized he was not only vulnerable, but losing ground. Temptations were more alluring, his values were under assault, and his strength was ebbing.

Isolated men are like sitting ducks for the devil. Yet many men are just like this Fort Worth transplant. Patrick Morley writes, "I think most men could recruit six pall-bearers, but hardly anyone has a friend he can call at 2:00 A.M."[66] Close friends are indispensable.

I encouraged my friend to begin asking God to provide strong men in his life and then begin putting himself in places where he could seek out their friendships—even if it meant changing churches. Several months later, God delivered and answered this man's prayer. Our Father has said He will supply our needs, and that includes friends, because men need men.

Don't try to box God in on this issue. He will provide what you need, but it will be on His schedule and according to His plan. Keep your eyes open and your ear to the ground. March in the direction He leads you, put yourself in a position to receive from Him, and He will honor His commitment to you.

But That's What Women Do

Whenever I hear or read about the need for men to get together, I wonder what it is we are supposed to do when we get together. We can't just sit around and talk, that's what women do. If you listen to the counsel of the day, it seems like we are supposed to meet and talk, read something, discuss what we've read, say whether or not we've been reading our Bible and praying, share our feelings, suggest prayer requests, pray, and then be better men because we got together.

While this is a fine plan, and one that men should seek to take advantage of, I believe some realism needs to be interjected into the discussion. As soon as this plan is put on the table, we have to make allowances for the challenge of masculinity. Most men are neither verbal nor intuitive. Even if we can put our finger on how it is we feel, articulating it is another matter. Confidentiality and trust are issues in any relationship, but there has to be something put on the table to be confidential and trustworthy with. I don't think most men are opposed to this idea of getting together, but we need to be pragmatic. Noteworthy relationships among men are typically not going to happen by Saturday night. You can't force friendship, and accountability among men is based upon honor and mutual respect, characteristics earned and proven over time. After all, a warrior wants to know the man he is trusting to look after his backside is going to be there when the enemy flanks him during the heat of battle.

If you watch, men spend a lot of time being together: standing, riding, walking, sitting, hunting, fishing, playing cards, throwing a ball around, golfing, or going somewhere. But they don't usually spend a lot of time talking. Men get to know one another by being together, not so much by talking together. Of course there are times—and must be—when men talk with one another, read together, argue, and pray. C.S. Lewis said, "You will not find the warrior, the poet, the philosopher or the Christian by staring in his eyes as if he were your mistress: better fight beside him, read with him, argue with him, pray with him."[67] A nice, neat, prescribed group fitting the passive, smiling, demure model often put forth, may not be the most fertile ground for men to feel secure with each other.

If a man's security is in Christ and with other men, then men need to agonize in the garden with their grieving brother, stand with their friends who are facing hardship, and lay their lives on the line with their buddy holding the high ground against the enemy. I think Jesus and the twelve had a lot of laughs about

Peter going under when he tried to walk on the water. I'll bet they argued politics when Simon, a zealot against the government, and Matthew, a government sub-contractor, traveled next to one another en route to the next town and pulled the other ten into their partisan debate. Like any group of men recounting a fight, can't you imagine the animated renditions of Jesus driving the money changers out of the temple as they sat around dinner that evening? Knowing how Jesus loved Lazarus, I'll bet they grieved with Him when He told them of Lazarus' death.

Jesus and His disciples were intense and passionate, not necessarily nice and neat with tidy relationships indicative of some placid painting. Like men, their relationships were sometimes aggressive, occasionally tender, frequently assertive, now and then rough, rugged, and humorous, but always honest. Men, we must realize our security is anchored in Christ, a real man, and with other men who will dare to be real men along with us, as genuine comrades in arms.

THE HONOR OF FRIENDSHIP

19

Bobb Biehl often tells young men, "Think more carefully about who you are with than what you do or where you do it. In the long run, the men around you will shape your life." A man's friends reflect who he is and influence what kind of man he will be. If a man's friend is doing his job, the man's family will be confident knowing "their man" is being looked out for. A man's friends believe in him. James 2:23 says Abraham believed in God, so God considered Abraham His friend forever. A man's friends solidify the confidence that comes with knowing he is secure.

Friendships of this caliber develop from respect, admiration, loyalty, dependability, and trust. While the Bible doesn't make a point of it, I'll bet these five qualities were present in Moses, Aaron, and Hur as they stood together surveying the progress of Israel's battle at Rephidim. These qualities must have laced their hearts together with a confidence not even Amalek could shake. Moses knew the gravity of the situation facing Israel, but he took the rod of God's power, two true friends, and set about climbing the hill to oversee the battle and lead the people God had entrusted into his care.

175

Brother, just like Israel's ongoing war against Amalek, we fight an ongoing war against our flesh. A secure man knows he is anchored in Christ, raises his hands to his Father as a sign of dependence, and relies upon the friendship of trusted brothers as he advances against the enemy and toward the promises of God. Stu Weber says, "I've often wondered how David's life would have been different had Jonathan lived. Had Jonathan been beside him, I doubt there would have been a Bathsheba episode."[68]

Respect, admiration, loyalty, dependability, and trust are crucial aspects of our character as men.

Respect

There is a measure of *respect* all men are afforded simply because they are men created in God's image, kind of a beginning balance to be wasted thoughtlessly or invested for growth. Then there is the respect that holds a man in high esteem because of what he has accomplished, his reputation, his countenance, or the way he treats those around him. Finally there is the respect that is earned and grows over time as a man's character comes to light. Watching a man deal with the struggles, failures, and hardships in his life, as well as his joys and successes, indicates how he will handle himself if you rely upon him to march alongside you on the road of life.

I prayed for more than ten years asking God to lead me to a group of men I could consider my close friends, men who would treasure my secrets, nourish my visions, launch my dreams with me, look out for my areas of vulnerability, support me when I was wounded, and confront me if I headed down the wrong road. He blessed me along the way with individuals who filled various aspects of what I was praying for, and then about three years ago He staked claim on my behalf to the richest mine of friendship I have ever experienced. Every Wednesday morning I meet with ten of the world's finest men, and I am blessed to call them my friends. We began with two simple tenets: honesty and confidentiality. I'll never forget the first morning we met and agreed to these two principles of conduct. Each premise was placed on the table, confidentiality first. In silence, each man nodded his head around the table. With that established, honesty was a natural by-product.

From the start, I respected the men of the SWAT (Spiritual Walking And Talking) team. Each is an accomplished man with an honorable reputation, a compelling countenance, and a determination to treat those around them with dignity. Each is committed to trust his Heavenly Father and run life's race with resolve. Each has pledged to love his family and show it by the manner in which he lives life.

Three years is a long time, and lots of water has flowed under the bridge. We have laughed a lot, cried some, argued a bit, grieved occasionally, counseled each other, carried on a great deal, and expressed our opinions convincingly. But we have always prayed together, been honest, and protected each other's secrets. The respect I have for these men now that I have seen them go through the fire is far different from the respect they garnered our first Wednesday based upon their accomplishments, reputations, and appearance. I would not hesitate to march against the gates of hell with these men. But perhaps most important of all, I believe with all my heart they would march to hell and back on my behalf if it was necessary.

Admiration

A man who is worthy to be counted as your friend is a man whom you *admire*. A friend has character qualities you can emulate and imitate, a man you want to be like, someone you would like your son or daughter to work for and model themselves after.

Years ago, a friend of mine introduced me to the writings of a sage old business consultant by the name of Peter Drucker. You may have read some of his books; he is the guru of business management. His book, *The Effective Executive,* is one of the most influential books I have read. With some regularity, I review my markings to remind myself of this man's wisdom. In his book, Mr. Drucker talks about going on a two-week personal retreat every August to take inventory of the past year. Has he achieved the goals he set last fall? If not, why not? What would he like to do in the upcoming year? What is it he can contribute that no one else around him can? How can he do that?

For several years now, I have imitated Mr. Drucker's annual retreat. Most years I am out of the office and out of town during the first week of November. I usually go to the mountains to refresh my soul, renew my spirit, and refocus on the important things in life. I take inventory of how I have lived for the past twelve months, assess my spiritual walk, examine the state of the important relationships in my life, and evaluate the overall health of my life. I make plans for how to correct course where necessary and set new goals for the next year. I write in my journal, read, sit and think, and meditate on apropropriate passages of God's Word. In so doing, my heart is healed and my spirit renewed.

Although I have never met Peter Drucker personally, the amazement of his wisdom and the wonder of his life challenge me to contemplate whether the same qualities can be part of my life. My admiration for him makes me want to emulate him and summon courage on a regular basis to evaluate my life for its effectiveness. Said simply, my admiration for Peter Drucker makes him one of my heroes.

A hero inspires us to greatness beyond what we thought possible. Heroes bring reality to our dreams. When a man stands next to a heroic man, he touches the potential of his own strength. Our heroes nurture the possibility that we may become heroic and inspire admiration in others. They make us better men and better friends.

Loyalty

Proverbs 17:17 says, "A brother is born for adversity." I don't know that *loyalty* is the most important aspect of friendship, but it is critical. My confidence grows if I know a loyal friend is pulling for me, will be there when I need him (even at his own expense), has my best interest at heart, and will keep my secrets between us and no one else. A loyal friend is bound by the honor between us.

After we have had a particularly revealing and candid discussion, one of my friends is fond of saying, "Pres, I appreciate your confidence. Our conversation goes no farther than our water glasses." And it doesn't. He is a loyal friend who I know has my interest placed above his own. I read recently,

> There are a few things even more important than life itself. Things such as keeping your word. Things such as holding to your promise. Things such as standing beside your brother. Things such as proving your friendship. Things such as staying and staying and staying...until you've given your all. Things such as being a loyal fellow-soldier—no matter what—even to the point of death.[69]

A loyal and tested friend gives me the confidence of knowing regardless of how deep the water gets, how hot the fire is, or how dry the desert, he will be beside me. A loyal friend is the last person to quit believing in you, the first person to encourage you, and the one who still likes the view even though he can see right through you.

Dependability

Dependability in a man who is your friend reassures you that you can count on him to do what is best for you.

In between Tres Piedras, New Mexico and Antonito, Colorado, Highway 285 passes by San Antonio peak, elevation 10,908 feet. It is a straight and lonely section of road running across high mountain prairie. A close friend and I were headed to Crested Butte to hike the trails, ride our mountain bikes, and eat Mexican food at Donita's Cantina in the evening. As we drove, Jared said, "Pres, I have something to ask you. I would like to tell Sarah (his wife) if I ever get headed in the wrong direction in life, and she can't get my attention, she should call you. If you are willing for her to do that, I would like for you to give me your word: If you ever get a call like that from her, no matter where you are or what you are doing, you will come to wherever I am and do whatever is necessary to get my attention. Will you pledge to do that for me?"

"Only upon one condition, Jared: that you will honor me with the same commitment."

That pledge still stands between Jared and me, and both Sarah and Dianne know about it. Jared and I have known each other for a long time. Obviously, this is not the kind of commitment you make with a nominal friend, but it is indicative of the dependability in a friend who helps a man know he is secure.

Trust

Trust is the confidence that continues to believe, even if what you believe appears to be untrue. To my way of thinking, trust is one step deeper than faith.

If I have $1,000 in my pocket, I can say I have faith God will provide for me no matter what. But if the $1,000 is whittled down to a dime, I will most likely alter my declaration and say I am trusting God to provide. I had faith in the first statement and exhibited trust in the second. Trust was a hypothetical possibility in the first statement, but in the second—with only ten cents to my name—it appears that God has not provided and my faith is in vain. When life gets down to that kind of a nub, trust enters the picture.

As faith is tested it becomes trust. Controlled belief seasons to become unreserved dependence. Self-sufficiency is laid aside for dependence.

Whether we are discussing your friend, "Joe," or your friend, God, trust is a critically important component in worthwhile friendships. Trust gives you the security of knowing your friend will be there in the most difficult times. It is the confidence that you can call your friend in the middle of the night and he will not hesitate to get out of bed and come to your side. Trust lets you know when the battle rages and it looks grim for the home team, your friend won't cut the other way and run. A trustworthy friend is one who believes your life is more important than his own. Weber writes, "A brother sticks. A brother doesn't make excuses and slip out the back door. A brother wades into the mess and crud and stands with you. And that's when you can tell your real friends."[70]

Lieutenant Worf

I was a fan of the science fiction television series, "Star Trek: The Next Generation." Captain Jean-Luc Picard and I have commanded the starship Enterprise through some mighty tough scrapes together. I didn't know if we were going to make it back from our encounter with the Borg, but we did. It took two episodes, but we prevailed. (I've been trying to convince our board of directors at the ministry that a uniform like Picard's would be appropriate for the president of the ministry, but so far they haven't caught the vision. I suppose it's slacks and button-downs until I can get it on the board's agenda again.)

Captain Picard's first officer is a commander by the name of Will Riker, and his chief of security is a lieutenant named Worf. In one particular episode, Riker is going to beam down to an alien planet and conduct a dangerous espionage mission. Ordinarily, the commander would have a contingent of officers from the starship to accompany him, but this is a personal mission, and thus he is planning to go alone. Just as Riker is putting the finishing touches on his camouflage face paint, Worf comes to his quarters, dressed in black, and announces he will accompany Riker to the surface of the planet. Riker carefully explains this is a personal mission and he is not obligated as security chief to go with him. Worf listens politely, nodding his head in agreement, then states, "Commander Riker, a warrior would never let his friend go into battle alone." A man with that attitude is a true friend.

The book you are reading has been on my mind for a long time, but it wasn't until I rearranged my responsibilities at the office that I began to make progress on actually getting it into your hands. In November of 1996, Dianne, Honey (the dog), and I left Fort Worth for Lyndonville, Vermont. I cut a deal with my dear friend, Dr. Fred Tomaselli, Executive Director of The Fold Family Ministries, if he would let us hide away at his place in northern Vermont to work on this manuscript I would minister to his staff 20 hours per week. Fred agreed, and the three of us spent an absolutely delightful month with Fred and Sally and the rest of the staff at The Fold. Dianne and I had never experienced a white Christmas, let alone a white Thanksgiving, but we had one in '96. Being in the northeast with snow on the ground, I felt like a real pilgrim. (Only instead of arriving on the Mayflower, we arrived on an American Airlines Super 80 via Hartford.)

The SWAT team pledged to pray for me as I began work in earnest outlining the manuscript you are reading. I asked Max, one of my SWAT team buddies, if I could share with you one of the faxes he sent while I was away. Max is a trustworthy man.

> Pres: It's Monday A.M. and ice with snow has crippled the Metroplex, and it's not even "Stock Show" time. There were only eight cars in our office parking lot at 8:30. I know that God will bless your time in Vermont because you're so "tuned in" to His Son.

Lamar tried to sit in your chair two Wednesdays ago and it just didn't work out. I'm thinking of asking Scott to banish him from the group if he tries it again. You will recall that James and John tried sort of the same thing with Jesus in wanting to sit at His right hand!

Pres, I'm praying specifically for the following: 1) That God will give you wisdom and sensitivity to mentoring the staff at The Fold ministry. 2) That God will use you to impact the kids at The Fold with your caring and love for them. 3) That God will knit your heart with Dianne's heart in a deeper way than you two have ever shared. That your marriage would reflect not only the "leaving and cleaving," but also the miraculous, mind-blowing love that Paul wrote the Ephesians about when he commanded the men to love their wives as Christ loved the church. I believe that Dianne will mirror that love right back to you. 4) That God will reveal His heart to you and transfer His passion into "His" manuscript through Pres Gillham.

Your SWAT team brother in Christ,

Max[71]

Like Worf said, a warrior never lets his friend go into battle alone. Max, the rest of the SWAT team, and several other close friends refused to let me go into battle by myself. They prayed for me, wrote me, faxed me, and e-mailed me their encouragement and support.

One of my perpetual trials in life is constant back pain. It is undiagnosed and has been with me for almost seventeen years. There are all sorts of things that cause the pain to increase, but one in particular is sitting. Consequently, you can imagine the physical pain associated with writing a book. Pain has been one area of vulnerability the devil has exploited during the composition of these pages, and he worked overtime while I was in Vermont.

Each afternoon, after I had sat all I could sit and my brain was fried from writing and fighting, I would lace up my boots, throw on a coat, grab my hat, and Honey and I would head to the woods. There we walked among the sugar maples and stood listening to the snow fall. I called out to my Father and trusted He would refurbish my aching soul and assuage the pain poking at me from the base of my skull to the tip of my tail bone. I fought the enemy's temptation to give up, to yield to the pain, to conclude the sacrifice was too great and sink toward disillusionment. I resisted his relentless declarations that God was not listening and the proof was in the pain. But often I thought of my friends who were standing by me, and my resolve was strengthened. Trust enables a man to count on his friends in the most difficult and vulnerable arenas of life.

A man was never intended to walk alone. Not even Jesus, the Son of God—a man's man—considered it wise to always be alone. Knowing how His Father created men, knowing His own experience, and being honor-bound by His word to never leave us or run out on us, we have confidence we are not alone. Recognizing this fosters great security, confidence, and hope, but we must also realize part of our Father's plan is for us to rely upon the strength of other men.

Both Jesus Christ and the apostle Paul knew and demonstrated how to depend upon their Heavenly Father for strength, even when facing death. Yet both valued knowing there was a trusted man to die beside them should the battle call for them to lay their lives down. As a man commissioned to fight in the same army, as a man fraught with fleshly vulnerability, as a man engaged in a great war against the devil and his angels, I need men around me who will support me, stand by me, look out for me, and if called upon to do so, lay their lives down on my behalf. A man's security is in Christ and with other men.

TED AND BILL AND JEAN-PIERRE

20

If you were to ask Jean-Pierre what he did for a living, I don't know that he would tell you he is a skinner. Technically, a skinner is one who drives draft animals, which is what Jean-Pierre does. He would probably say, "Aye, I do a bits of dis and a bits of dat, and am honored to do it with me family and me friends." By "family" he would mean his dad, Laurent, and by "friends" he would mean Ted and Bill, his two draft horses, who happen to be his best friends.

I was privileged to be working and ministering again with The Fold Family Ministries. Ted and Bill—with Jean-Pierre at the reins—had pulled The Fold staff on its annual sleigh ride along the Canadian border through the sugar maple forests, past bears' dens, beside sugar shacks where the famous Vermont maple syrup is boiled and bottled, and safely back to the barn. Pulling a sleigh of thirty people for an hour seemed all in a day's work for Ted and Bill, but the steam poured off of their 2,300-pound bodies as they showed us a wonderful side of New England that would have gone otherwise unnoticed.

While Ted and Bill were unhitched and taken to the barn, the staff retreated from the sleet and snow into a split-wood warming house for cider, coffee, rolls, and samples of the various grades of maple syrup. Being fascinated by the horses, and enjoying the cold, inclement weather, this Texas boy stayed outside to talk with Jean-Pierre. As he tended to Ted and Bill they stood with their noses pressed tightly together and one each of their rear legs cocked in a resting position. They seemed oblivious to the worsening weather and impending storm.

While he unhitched their harnesses, Jean-Pierre talked about the teamwork-dynamic of draft horses. Deciphering Jean-Pierre's French-Canadian-northern-Vermonter dialect into Texas drawl, here is what I learned: If Ted is hitched to a load by himself, the maximum weight he is capable of pulling can ultimately be determined. Let's call that weight "x." Next, we do the same with Bill and call the maximum weight he is capable of pulling "y." After everybody has had time to rest and recuperate, Ted and Bill are hitched together where they work side-by-side as a team. Weight is added and they begin to pull. When all is said and done, the weight Ted and Bill pull together is "x" plus "y," doubled, plus half again more! In other words, let's say each horse is capable of pulling 4,000 pounds by himself. Together, they can pull *24,000 pounds.*

Look how much more effective Ted and Bill are as a team, and when they are done working, they get to stand with their noses together. (This is truly a great arrangement.) This is probably not all that different from what God had in mind in Ecclesiastes 4:12 when He said, "A cord of three strands is not quickly torn apart." He may well have been contemplating this when He devised the body of Christ, and it may be the impetus behind His invention of friendship. It is probably why He looked at Adam and said, "You know what? This is not a good plan for man to be alone. Let's see, I need to create…" And He devised a new plan.

Trusting Christ to express His life through us is an individual responsibility each man carries, but our responsibility does not stop there. We—the body of Christ—have a responsibility to trust Christ *together* as well. And if we do so, Ted and Bill present a picture of what is possible.

If I trust my Father and depend upon Him as my source of strength, I demonstrate what a true man is. If we collectively depend upon our Father as our source of strength, we demonstrate who men are. A strong man marching beside other strong men advances an army in league with our majestic God, against which the world, the devil, and his hordes wither.

The Secret of Alexander's Invincibility

Epaminondas was the Thebean general and statesman who defeated the Spartan army at Leuctra and Mantinea. Philip II, who reigned as king of Macedon from 359–336 B.C., knew this great man, and from the knowledge gained during their relationship he created the Macedonian war machine his son, Alexander the Great, would wield with such effectiveness it never lost a battle or siege.

At the core of his military strategy, Alexander employed three primary elements: the archers, the infantry, and the cavalry. The archers were used in ancient times as artillery is used today, while the cavalry was used like the modern army uses armored divisions. Tactically, the infantry has changed the least. Each man is still responsible for the man beside him, the two of them are responsible to their unit, and the unit is responsible to the whole. Individually and collectively, depending upon the training and determination of the other, they march forward, pushing the enemy backward, protecting one another with each assault from the enemy's arsenal, gaining victory with each step, conquering with each sector taken, succeeding with each act of courage, and celebrating triumph through relentless interdependence.

The Macedonian army, under the command of Alexander, was organized into six groups of approximately 2,000 troops each that marched in a tight rank and file formation called a phalanx.

Each warrior in the phalanx had a trusted companion who guarded his vulnerable right side, and the phalanx itself had shield bearers on the right flank to guard their collective weak side. Alexander, who quite frequently led the cavalry charge in an oblique-angle attack from the right flank of the infantry, was guarded by archers who shot their missiles into the enemy in advance of his cavalry's attack.

The left flank of the Macedonian phalanx was commanded by the brilliant tactician Parmenion, one of Alexander's closest friends. The cavalry and archers on the left wing were charged with occupying the enemy's opposing wing and preventing them from harming the continuity of the phalanx, which was charged with shocking the center of the enemy line.

There is more to these paragraphs than a simple discourse on Macedonian military strategy. Warrior A is responsible for protecting the vulnerability of warrior B; together they are responsible for their unit's effectiveness, and their unit works together to make the phalanx effective. The shield bearers guarded the weakness of the phalanx on the right, and as Alexander's offensive cavalry charged from the right wing, the archers guarded the safety of the assault. The defensive cavalry strengthened the phalanx from the left while being assisted by the missilery on the left. In combination, the infantry, the cavalry, and the missilery under the command of Alexander was indomitable.

The modern military has sophisticated weaponry like Alexander couldn't imagine in his wildest dreams. Alexander's cavalry hadn't even invented stirrups for their saddles, let alone dreamed of flying machines launching missiles orientated by lasers sensitive enough to guide them down ventilator shafts into command bunkers. And yet one thing hasn't changed in the slightest from antiquity to modernity: The interdependence that made Alexander's army invincible is still relentlessly disciplined into the mind of every recruit who dons a military uniform. The man on your right looks out for you, you look out for the man on your left, and he looks out for the man on his left while depending on the man to his right. You fight together, share together, march together, and if called upon to do so, die together. Men depending upon trustworthy men who will guard their weaknesses and march with them toward a shared victory is still an unbeatable combination.

Just as the genius of Alexander guided his Macedonian phalanx to victory over Darius at Gaugamela, the incomparable genius of Jesus Christ, our commander, leads us toward victory on the battlefields that engage us. A man's security is in Christ and with other men. Developing friendships of this sort isn't going to happen quickly. Trustworthy relationships are often forged in the foundry of difficulty and the relentlessness of time. But this simply points definitively to the importance of close friendships.

As you begin to trust your Heavenly Father to supply men of this caliber in your life, you must tap Him as the source of your true strength and not forget that your security fundamentally resides in Christ. It is only from this vantage point you can muster the courage to reveal yourself to others and see where your Father is leading the relationship.

Allowing time to take its course, and your Father to guide the development of these crucial relationships, the Spirit will guide you toward your ultimate goal of being honest and transparent with your trusted friend. This nurtures two essential elements of friendship: First, by trusting your friend with the treasures of your heart you promote his trust, confidence, and transparency in return. Second, you want your friend to have enough information about you to notice if something is wrong in your life. Reliable men entrusted with the classified contents of a friend's heart know they have the responsibility to guard their buddy's weakness and strengthen his defenses. This enhances the security we have in Christ. Lewis says,

> For a Christian, there are, strictly speaking, no chances. A secret Master of the Ceremonies has been at work. Christ, who said to the disciples "Ye have not chosen me, but I have chosen you," can truly say to every group of Christian friends, "You have not chosen one another but I have chosen you for one another." The Friendship is not a reward for our discrimination and good taste in finding one another out. It is the instrument by which God reveals to each the beauties of all the others. They are no greater than the beauties of a thousand other men; by Friendship God opens our eyes to them. They are, like all beauties, derived from Him, and then, in a good Friendship, increased by Him through the Friendship itself, so that it is His instrument for creating as well as for revealing. At this feast it is He who has spread the board and it is He who has chosen the guests. It is He, we may dare to hope, who sometimes does, and always should, preside. Let us not reckon with our Host.[72]

How vividly I remember the Wednesday morning one of my SWAT team buddies came into the kitchen of the sixth-floor office where we meet with a message to deliver. As he kissed his wife good-bye and headed for the garage, she said, "Tell all the guys I love them."[73] Of course, we laughed and carried on, but each of us knew what she meant, and we knew each of our wives would say exactly the same thing. We are better men because we are secure in Christ and secure with each other. And it has not escaped the notice of our wives that they are the beneficiaries of this masculine security.

Finding Friendship

Peter Drucker says, "In a knowledge area there are no superiors or subordinates, there are only older and younger men."[74] The implication is that competition to establish dominance between peers is counterproductive. Recognizing the need of a man to have the influence of other men in his life, Mr. Drucker is asserting that productivity will be generated by turning the energy of competition into the transfer of wisdom and knowledge. In whatever areas of life men have common goals, they will benefit from having a mentor.

Mr. Drucker also implies older men have more wisdom and knowledge than younger men do, and that is true for the most part. Provided he has been paying attention and learning the lessons of history, an older man has more experience to draw from. However, one of the fundamental errors we can make in life is to assume younger men do not have anything to contribute to our lives that will be beneficial. Such an attitude promotes isolation and nurses self-pride, two things not indicative of a man who knows who he is, where his strength emanates from, and that he is secure in Christ.

I must admit, I have some skepticism about how functional accountability groups and assigned mentors are, not because they are bad ideas, but because they have unrealistic expectations placed on them. Just because the principle is valid, doesn't necessarily mean a confidant and trusted friend can be dispensed from a sign-up sheet. On the other hand, I'm all for stepping into the batter's box and swinging. If you don't ever take the risk of striking out you can never hope to hit the ball. As I've said already, don't expect the type of relationship we are discussing to happen quickly. Just because you join a Sunday School class, organize a sharing group, start meeting two other guys for breakfast each week, or begin pouring your heart and soul out to the guy in the cube next to you doesn't mean you will find a true and trustworthy friend. Rome wasn't built in a day and neither is friendship—but don't let that deter you. Friendship is essential and God will provide!

Trust your Heavenly Father. Tell Him about your needs and pour your heart out to Him. Share your struggles and doubts and victories and confidences with Him. In His time, He will provide exactly what you need. He is honor-bound to do so.[75] Until He decides the time is right in your life for a friend like we have been talking about, strengthen yourself in the Lord, your Heavenly Father, just as David did in 1 Samuel 30.

In the meantime, armed with this dose of reality, involve yourself in the men's group at church, join a Promise Keeper's organization, start studying God's Word with a couple of guys, or begin praying with your fishing buddy. As long as your expectations are reasonable, trying things of this sort isn't going to hurt anything. So you read a book together and don't find a soulmate, keep swinging and trusting your Father. After all, you've lost nothing. You have trusted your Father and shared your heart.

Let me encourage you to be an initiator. This doesn't mean you dump all your goods on the table at the drop of a hat. Be wise and exercise moderation, but push the envelope a little as well. Remember, you are secure in Christ.

What happens in a worst-case scenario? Let's say you determine your golfing buddy is a man who you'd like to share your heart with on a deeper level than golf. He is a believer, walks with the Lord, reads the Word, and is growing in His faith. You are sitting at the seventh tee waiting on some duffers to find their scattered balls, not one of which is on the fairway (at least not the seventh fairway). Seizing the moment, and believing you are being led by the Spirit, you broach a subject that is on your heart. It is a knottier problem than you two have ever shared before, and your confidence isn't handled well.

If you listen closely, you will hear the Holy Spirit yelling "Fore" toward your heart's ear because the devil is about to shank one in your direction. If you are not on your toes, you will buy into his lines about embarrassment, accusations about your stupidity and miscalculation, vows to never do that again as long as you live, inappropriate apologies, and anger toward God for causing you such discomfort. It's baloney. All of it is the devil's crock of lies correlated with your unique version of the flesh.

You don't have to go along with his stuff.[76] You are a new man in Christ who is secure, even though you don't feel like it. Set your mind on the truth, thank God you know how far your friendship goes with your golfing buddy, and get back to all of those snide remarks you were making about duffers. After all, you're next on the tee.

Your job is not to find a friend. Your job is to be the man God has called you to be. Depend on Him as your strength, source, significance, and security and keep sharing your heart. He will bring you a friend in His time and afford you the privilege of being a friend in the meantime.

Being an Influential Friend

Remember one truth: A warrior doesn't lay his life down for what he can get out of the experience; he lays it down because he is committed to a cause. He lays it down because his allegiance is to a noble ideal. He lays it down because others will benefit by his doing so. He lays it down because he knows his heart is not his own—long ago he gave his heart and life to his Father. He knows, as Jim Elliot said, "He is no fool who gives what he cannot keep to gain what he cannot lose."[77]

No matter how difficult the task of friendship might be, mentoring is not only about finding someone who can encourage you and stand by you when life is rocking and rolling. Mentoring is also about sharing your life, and quite often the simplest things are the most profound.

Preston McCann was an all-conference football player at East Central State College in Oklahoma, the alternate center and linebacker on the All-Oklahoma team, superintendent of schools at Beggs, Oklahoma, principal of Franklin School in Okmulgee, Oklahoma, my dad's best friend, and the man I was named after. He died at age 53 of melanoma and was remembered as a kind and generous man by people all over the state. Even though I was young when he died, I still have vivid memories of him. One in particular stands out.

Mr. McCann had a gray bull named Cochise that he admired and I revered. Whenever Dad and I went to visit, Mr. McCann would initiate a trip to the barn to see his bull. I would climb up on the rail fence so I could be eye-to-eye with Cochise, Mr. McCann, and Dad. In that setting, while watching and admiring the monstrous gray bull, I was included in a simple part of Mr. McCann's life. I listened to Dad and him talk and tell stories and laugh. I listened to him tell me about Cochise and watched him work with the great animal. But most of all, I felt I was part of Mr. McCann's life and Dad's friendship with him. Cochise was the entrée, catalyst, and forum around which our relationships grew.

In my keepsake box I have a gray, plastic bull named Cochise. He has been in there for almost forty years. Isn't it odd that of all the toys of childhood, one of the most important is connected to a man who included me in a simple part of his life? How well I remember the day Mr. McCann explained to me Cochise didn't have any horns because he had cut them off. I didn't really understand why a man would cut the horns off of his bull, but guess what? At my insistence, and with great ceremony, Dad and I de-horned my bull as well, and then we put a little Merthiolate on each side of his plastic head. When I showed him, Mr. McCann was proud and examined my bull closely, finally pronouncing him the exact replica of Cochise.

It's a little thing—a toy bull—but my dad's best friend included me in an important part of his life, and even though I was only a preschooler, I felt the honor and still remember it. Based on the stories Dad tells about Preston McCann, I have concluded he was a great man. Even though he died when I was young, I have been influenced and blessed by his life. I sometimes wonder, thinking about the plastic, de-horned bull in my keepsake box, how great Mr. McCann would be in my eyes if he had never stood beside me admiring and talking about his de-horned bull, Cochise.

He was a busy, influential man of reputation and I was just a small boy, but exerting influence to a world larger than your own is a blessing you must not waste, just as he did not. Sharing your life with others taps into the fundamental makeup of a man. We are providers and protectors, warriors fighting for a noble cause, modern day heroes up against evil odds. Our enemy fell from heaven[78] and is now thrashing about on earth looking for people to destroy in an effort to get even with God. We stand in his path.

This is your place as a man. It's where you belong. This is where a man who is depending upon his Father and standing shoulder-to-shoulder with other men is most secure. This is where the boys of today will learn to take their place as the men of tomorrow. When a man chooses to abdicate, thinking he will gain security by so doing, he is chasing a fickle deception, pouring his life down a hole, disgracing his manhood. A real man demonstrates strength through dependence, realizes security through Christ, and marches beside strong men. A real man lays his life down for the noble cause and does so with honor. A real man would have it no other way.

Will You or Won't You?

Men take responsibility for themselves, for other men, for their family and friends, for those within their sphere of influence, and for those less fortunate. A man takes the life his Father has given him and passes it on to others through a continual act of blessing, self-sacrifice, friendship, and mentoring. Through this ritual of life a man demonstrates manhood and passes the mantle of masculinity to those closest to him. If a man lives a life of independence and insecurity, he fails in his task as a man.

We can talk all day about friendship and mentoring, but you can readily see these wonderful, biblical concepts and ideas depend upon you, and other men around you, trusting Christ as life and depending upon God as Father. Will you trust your Father, or won't you? Will the man you are standing next to in life trust his Father, or won't he?

As we have already discussed, there are many men who have failed to have the mantle of masculinity passed to them. Their dad dropped the ball. As a result, they doubt their masculinity and are searching for security and masculine status in all the wrong places: women, work, recreation, achievement, or pleasure. But only Christ can shore up a sagging, masculine self-esteem. Even at their best, these various aspects of life—including friendships with other men—are not sufficient to anchor a man as a corner post should be anchored. Christ alone can bring the blessing of masculinity to a man fighting for his masculine identity.

There are other men who take a mental inventory of their masculine storehouse and conclude they are masculine. Like me, they bequeathed the honor on themselves. They believe their manhood is well established based upon their experience and the support structures around them. But true masculinity, real strength, and *bona fide* security are not based upon experience, support structures, accomplishments, bank accounts, positions, or battles won. Any avenue for trying to gain masculinity other than the one mapped by our Father in heaven is charted by the flesh and circumvents God's divine plan.

A weak and insecure man is a man who fails to depend upon his Father for strength and attempts to derive security some- where other than in Christ Jesus. The world may look at such a man and evaluate his accomplishments, net worth, deeds for mankind, address, or make of his suit and conclude he is a strong, secure man. But such an evaluation is based upon tem- poral values and earthly wisdom. A real man looks to the blessing of his Father and a vision of the future to derive strength and security. Earthly wisdom based upon apparent strength is deception. God's wisdom based upon real strength is security.

As men we all start from the same place and are governed by the same design. It does not matter how you feel about your masculinity or what your conclusions are regarding your manhood. Your Father has pronounced His blessing and declared you a man. Your response is to trust Him and depend upon Him.

Deep in your soul you thrive on your Father's blessing and you want to depend upon Him. The new heart He has given you resonates with the strength and security derived from Him. Regardless of whether your history has proven productive or unproductive, your heart's desire is to act like a man whose strength, significance, and security are anchored in Him.

It is true, if asked to do so, a man can—and must at times—stand alone. In His wisdom, God has made provision for this by filling us with His Spirit and placing us in league with Jesus Christ. There is no doubt about it—we are secure in Him and He is our source.

But God's master plan is for us to stand with other men who are anchored in Christ. When men stand together, mutually depending upon their Heavenly Father, they are more effective. A corner post can stand by itself, but it is more secure if there are three posts tied together. I'm confident that each soldier in Alexander's army was capable of standing alone and defending himself. However, the success of the Macedonian army was not independence but interdependence.

A real man knows his security is in Christ and with other men, and a real man would have it no other way.

FAILURE AND RECOVERY

21

"I don't know who you are talking about! Leave me alone, I tell you. I don't know anything about the man!" There was loud cursing and swearing like you have never heard before—that is, unless you have been present when a man is being tortured to tell what he knows.

Is this the scene from the back room in a gang hide out? A drug deal gone sour? Is this poor, wretched soul stretched across an electrified, wire-spring mattress frame sweating like a pig on a spit as the switch is thrown for a few seconds of muscle-contorting atrocity? On the contrary. This tortured man is free to come and go as he pleases. He is warming himself by a courtyard fire to quell the evening chill and his interrogators are two girls—not women, girls—servant-girls asking innocent, curious questions.

Not many men have to live with a failure like Peter's. Not many have their failure recorded four different times in the world's all-time, runaway, best-selling book.[79] Few of us have committed failures that are the subject of so many sermons of derision, designed to motivate listeners to lives of diligence because of a poor example.

And, in all honesty, there are not many men called "Rock," especially after they have committed as dastardly a denial as Peter did standing in the courtyard during Christ's trial before the high priest. Those men who break under the duress of torture realize they have failed, but at least they have failed in extreme circumstances. Peter's failure did not afford him that luxury, and the Scriptures speak to this fact. They leave us with a broken, humiliating failure of courage that is summed up with these words in Matthew 26:75: "And he went out and wept bitterly."

A man who is broken by his failure, who runs through the streets wailing, is a man grieving his weakness and mourning the loss of his honor. Proverbs 24:10 states simply, "If you are slack in the day of distress, your strength is limited." There is no sight more unsettling than watching a tormented man languish under the excruciating pain of his own failure. The strength that made him proud met its match in the failure he committed. This weakness may as well be a rack, torturing him toward the death of his soul.

Brother, you are going to experience failure. Christianity is not a magic mantra invoking divine protection from the harshness of life or the consequences of fleshly choices. This is a war, a spiritual war, and there will be casualties.

When failure occurs, how does a man handle it? I want to explore seven steps for recovering from failure, and point out clearly that failure is not always the result of sin. Just because things are going poorly and you conclude your efforts have failed, does not necessarily mean you walked after the flesh. Evaluating results can be a tricky business.

There are plenty of successes achieved by the force of a man's will and determination to succeed, but our Father declares them failures because they were generated by fleshly resolve. On the other hand, there are those results that appear to be failures, and that feel like failures, but which our Father declares successes because we trusted Him. In other words, God evaluates success versus failure based upon methodology rather than results.[80] However, God will always use results—especially unpleasant ones—to speak to our hearts about His plans.

One final word before we begin the seven steps: Don't be afraid of failure, be afraid of not trying. I remind you of Teddy Roosevelt's words, "Far better it is to dare mighty things, to win glorious triumphs even though checkered by failure, than to take rank with those poor spirits who neither enjoy much nor suffer much because they live in the gray twilight that knows neither victory nor defeat."[81]

What of those times when failure is your own doing? You walked after the flesh and lived independently. It seemed like a reasonable course to pursue at the time, but now, as you gaze back across your trail, you see only disaster. You blew it. You have sinned and the consequences are staring you in the face. What do you do?

Repent

The first step in recovering from failure is to *repent*. Acknowledge you blew it. Own up to the fact you walked after the flesh, bought the enemy's temptation, behaved contrary to who you really are, and misrepresented yourself and your Father. A secure man apologizes. He apologizes to his Heavenly Father and to anyone affected by his choice to betray his manhood and walk after the flesh.

Here is a critical rule that applies when apologizing to others: Private failures require private apologies, public failures require public apologies. To whatever extent your sin was public, that is the extent to which your apology goes. Repentance is not a theological tool for making you feel better and erasing your failure. Repentance means owning up to your failure and turning away from it with the intent of going in another direction. Anything less than this is not true repentance. Furthermore, just because you repent does not mean the consequences of your failure will be resolved.

This begs the question, "Why should I repent if I'm not going to escape the consequences?" Answer: Because you don't want to stay in your sin and continue down the wrong road. You are a man—you have a new heart that wants to be in tune with your Father's heart. Real men don't weasel around the consequences of failure. If you attempt an end run around repentance, the honor of masculinity will be sacrificed. It will seem as though your masculinity has lost its face and its dignity. A secure man—which you are in Christ, and hopefully the brothers who stand with you in times such as this are as well—repents and apologizes when necessary.

Apologies are specific. "I'm sorry if…" is a worthless apology. Determine what you did and apologize specifically for doing it as well as for the fallout it caused.

Refocus

The second step is to *refocus* on what you know. This is what the Bible calls setting your mind.[82] It is to be done with resolute determination and repetitious effort while depending upon your Father for strength.

Remember, your *story* is about a great battle between God and the devil. Your heart wants to engage with your Father's heart against the enemy forces in what has proven to be the classic struggle between good and evil where you are the potential hero. While it is true you have just taken an enemy strike, you have the training and resources to refocus on the truth.

Here is what you know:

- Your *strength* is realized through depending on your Heavenly Father.

- You are accepted and forgiven in Christ who is your *source* and constant companion. He is your marching partner in the phalanx of spiritual warfare.

- Your *significance* is not in how well you perform but is anchored in Christ.

- Your *security* is in Him and with other men who will help you guard your heart and look out for your weakness. This means you are free to be yourself and stand with masculine confidence.

- And by your Father's grace, you will hold your *station* in life until further notice.

These facts must be etched into your mind and written on your heart. It is imperative you refocus on what you know. Regardless of why failure comes, a man must return to the essential fundamentals, regain his bearings, and refocus on the truth.

Remind

The third step in recovering from failure is to *remind* yourself what your station in life is. A man is a corner post, anchored in the solid rock of Jesus Christ and tied together with other men. Your position is carrying out redemption and blessing.

Renew

Fourth, in order to recover from failure a man must *renew* his resolve to accomplish his Father's calling. This step often feels like an opportune time for personal resolutions, vows, and promises, and the devil will tempt you to conclude these, which will renew the call of God in your life. But self-strength is weakness and a perversion of true masculinity. From the day God first created Adam, the message of masculinity has been clear: Manhood is about dependence.

God is not interested in what you can do for Him. No matter how productive your flesh, no matter how iron-clad your will, no matter how determined you are to produce something for God, He simply is not that poor. Don't buy the enemy's lie asserting you can live the Christian life through determination and promises. Besides being impossible, it is an affront to your Father and is contrary to the lifestyle exemplified by your elder brother, Jesus, the perfect man.

Your Father never intended you to live the Christian life in your own power because it is not your life to live. It is Christ's life to live. Your call is to allow Him to live His life in you and through you. It is to trust Him by depending upon your Father. Give life your best shot with these tenets as your rallying cry.[83]

As I sat down to write today I had two prayers to choose from: On the one hand I could pray, "Dear Father, as I prepare to begin writing today, I ask You to help me. Amen." On the other hand, I could pray, "Dear Father, as I prepare to begin writing today, I trust You to express yourself through my personality, talents, and gifts to say what is on Your heart. Amen." While these two prayers are similar, they are far from synonymous. To implore God to help me implies I have ability apart from Him. If He were to opt out of helping me, there would still be the possibility a successful work of literature could be produced. The second prayer acknowledges dependence and presumes a determination on my part to trust Him and not my own resources. The first prayer is a prayer anchored in the strength of the flesh and is not indicative of real masculinity. The second prayer is anchored in Christ and dependence upon the Father. This prayer renews my determination to hold my station in life.

Don't get me wrong, both prayers may yield literary work that communicates effectively. However, there is one problem: That is not the goal. The goal is to depend upon my Father and be a strong man. Writing the book is secondary in importance.

From this perspective, the glory as well as the responsibility is my Father's. The satisfaction and joy of a job well done is ours to share as a Father-son team. Failure is always a signal flare reminding us to renew our resolve to be strong men who are dependent upon our Father.

Recover

The fifth step in the process is to *recover*. Depending on the intensity of your failure, this may not happen quickly. Recovery is a unique process defying prescription, but here are some of the ways I recover from failure. Nearly every night I put a leash on my dog and go for a walk. Sometimes it is short and sometimes long, but often it serves as a recovery period. I think and pray about the things weighing me down, and when I step back through the door of my house, recovery has been facilitated. I also ride my bicycle. Most of the time I ride for cardiovascular benefit, but occasionally I ride for therapy. If multiple things have closed in on me, I pack up my fly rod and head for the river, or I slip into my hiking boots and disappear into the woods for a few hours. Time alone, reflecting on my life with God, does wonders for recovery.

One Friday evening several months ago Dianne and I got into a less than pleasant discussion (read: had a fight) about something I can't remember now. (I'm sure it was of national and strategic importance, like whether she had gotten the oil changed in her truck or not, or maybe it pertained to which Italian restaurant to eat at. The point is, we were not happy campers.) We got our predicament sorted out, kissed and made up, and went to bed. I'm sure you have noticed apologizing, kissing and making up, hugging, and forgiving do wonderful things for the mind but rarely sink in deep enough—at least right away—to calm the emotion associated with failure. Dianne and I were fine by the time we turned the lights out on our fight, but my emotions were still simmering.

I woke up about 4:00 A.M., tried all the tricks, but couldn't go back to sleep. So I got up and went outside to sit in the front yard and listen to the mockingbird sing. There was a full moon in the western sky illuminating the yard almost as effectively as the street lamp on the corner. I set my lawn chair on the front walk, angled so I could see the moon, and began sorting through my residual emotions. And then this thought came to me: *I wonder how far west I could drive before the moon disappeared below the horizon?*

It was Saturday morning. Dianne was going to a baby shower. I mowed the grass two days earlier. Why not?

I left Di a note and backed our car down the drive. I turned north on Forest Park, left on the Rosedale access road, and accelerated onto I-30 heading west toward Abilene with the full moon shining through my windshield. Within ten minutes the rolling prairies from which Fort Worth had grown surrounded my car, and the lights of Cowtown began dimming in my rearview mirror.

In case anyone asks you, the moon sets in Ranger, Texas, or at least it did that morning. I stopped at a café in Ranger for eggs and bacon and toast (this is the place where the waitresses call you "Hon"), then turned my car east toward home. En route I stopped beside the Brazos River just west of Weatherford and I walked along the sand bank in my sandals for a mile or so, sitting down to listen as the waters discussed their inexorable route to the Gulf of Mexico.

I prayed some, and thought some, and listened a lot. I sat, and I walked, and I felt the warm sand flip up on the back of my calves. But most of all I recovered from the failure of the night before. Time away, reflecting on God's work in our lives, gives perspective and allows healing to begin.

Review

The sixth step in recovering from failure is to *review* what went wrong. What was the devil's strategy and how did he accomplish his goal? What could you have done to catch his temptations and resist him? Consider two passages from Paul to the church at Corinth. In 2 Corinthians 7:9-11, he writes, "I now rejoice, not that you were made sorrowful, but that you were made sorrowful to the point of repentance; for you were made sorrowful according to the will of God, in order that you might not suffer loss in anything through us. For the sorrow that is according to the will of God produces a repentance without regret, leading to salvation; but the sorrow of the world produces death. For behold what earnestness this very thing, this godly sorrow, has produced in you: what vindication of yourselves, what indignation, what fear, what longing, what zeal, what avenging of wrong!" Then in 10:5 he adds, "We are destroying speculations and every lofty thing raised up against the knowledge of God, and we are taking every thought captive to the obedience of Christ."

In this case, the readers had a failure in their lives requiring repentance. Sorrow was good in that it led them to a point of genuine determination to turn away from their fleshly pursuit. As they review what went wrong there is indignation—"I can't believe I bought that lie from the enemy. The coward attacked me while I wasn't looking!" There is also fear, not in the sense of terror, but in the sense of respect: "I've got to hand it to him, he is a cunning adversary." There is longing: "Father, I do not want to live life this way. It is contrary to Your plan and a violation of my heart." And there is zeal: "Father, it is my determination to say, 'No!' to the devil's temptation and trust You to fill me with the power of Your Spirit."

Paul writes that he is destroying anything opposed to what he knows to be true about his Father, most of which is mere speculation by the devil, and he is taking every one of these thoughts captive in order to live life as a man obedient to Jesus Christ.

After things have calmed down and you have stopped your emotional slide—in other words, as you are on your way back from Ranger—avenge the wrong. Turn the tables on the devil and use your failure to your benefit and your Father's glory. Said another way, learn from your mistake. What fleshly pattern did the enemy tap into? How did he attack you? At what point did you buy his speculation, lie, or temptation, consider it true, and act on it? That is the point at which you sinned. Remember, temptation becomes sin when you accept it as a viable plan. Until then it is simply the devil doing his song and dance with your flesh.

Once you determine the point at which you bought the lie, identify it as the critical juncture where failure was born. Verbalize to yourself the correct response you should have made. Learn from your failure. See yourself saying, "No! I'm not going along with that. I'm a new man with a new heart. I am free—and obliged—to say, 'No! Get behind me Satan, you're blocking my view.'"[84]

In reviewing what went wrong you build a repository of skills for combating the enemy's temptations, and you do it at his expense. Nothing garners more confidence than experience. A secure man who recovers from failure is a confident man—confident in who he is as a new man in Christ, and confident in who his Father is.

Reward

The seventh step in recovering from failure is to experience the *reward* of maturity. As you are diligent to capitalize on this circumstance, you will experience that reward. Your consistency in walking in the power of the Spirit will increase, you will see more consonant victory over your fleshly patterns, your confidence in your Father's plan will grow, and your ability to communicate your life to others will be facilitated.

22

LIVING A COURAGEOUS LIFE

Almost twenty years ago, a man I know called his family together, lined them up in the family room, and beginning with Katy, the four-year-old, told each of them he didn't need them in his life. Last in line was his shell-shocked wife. "I don't need you. I don't love you. I'm leaving. The divorce papers will arrive in a few days."

And with that, he left to sleep in the arms of a younger woman and seek personal fulfillment through irresponsibility. His statement to the family as he turned tail to run is very revealing. He thought life was about other people taking care of him, and defined his masculinity by going to bed with another woman. That man either missed or ignored the fact that God intended a man to be an instrument of redemption who lays his life down rather than picks it up.

Katy latched onto me in her dad's absence. While just a young man, I knew enough to recognize she was missing him and had chosen me as a surrogate. I didn't know much about being a dad, and with three brothers I sure didn't know anything about little girls, but Katy reached out to me, and as best I knew how, I reached back. Twenty years later I have a file folder full of

Father's Day cards signed, "I love you, Katy," and just a few months ago I performed her wedding to a remarkable young man who committed himself to love her until death parted them.

One winter, Katy came down for a visit. Even though we had spent a lot of time together, this was her first trip to Fort Worth without her mom. As the time of her arrival approached, I grew a little apprehensive about what to do for several days with a teenage girl. There would be time with my wife and time with my family and time with my brothers, but I knew Katy and I needed time together. I planned a few fun things, but mostly I determined to do the things I normally do and take Katy with me.

On Saturday morning we ate a big breakfast and then put on our warm clothes for a hike near Rocky Creek and the railroad trestle. It was a cold, blustery day, which caused me to think twice about taking Katy to the woods with me, but the rationale for heading out went like this: *Katy admires me as a man and needs to be part of my life. She needs to understand what I do, how I think, what I enjoy, and where I hide out when I need a respite. She needs to be included in my life and believe she can communicate with me. She needs to be cared for when she enters into my world. If Katy were not here, I would be heading for the woods and relishing the fact that the weather has turned cantankerous.* So off we went.

We crossed through the pastures, crawled through the barbed wire fence rows, wound our way through the cottonwood thicket, jumped a few rabbits, flushed two or three coveys of quail, saw a bobcat—the only one I have ever seen in the wild—and sat in the sun under the railroad trestle and talked about all kinds of nothing. I took her to my secret spot, had her sit down in my place, and told her about the day I was sitting there, perfectly concealed from an approaching coyote. I got down on my hands and knees eight feet away to show her where the coyote was when he finally noticed me. I looked at her like he looked at me, and tried to describe what those few magical seconds were like when we locked eyes. Further along we saw where the deer had bedded down for the night, trailed after some coon tracks by the creek, and picked some dried weeds for a table arrangement on our way back to the car.

Katy and I finished the weekend together and I put her back on the plane for home. It was then I began to second-guess myself and the decision I had made to include her in my normal routine rather than "entertain" her. The doubts didn't last long. I talked with Katy's mom two days later and she told me Katy had a great trip, and she had especially enjoyed Saturday's hike to the trestle.

A courageous man serves as Christ served, laying his life down on behalf of those He loves. This may mean stepping into the line of fire, but it can also mean sharing your heart and soul with transparent honesty, or sitting in the sun under the trestle on a cold, Saturday morning.

Life: Lay It Down

Time is life, and giving your time is like giving your life. A courageous man knows the importance of taking those he loves with him through life. Manhood is a code of honor, an ethic of integrity, a lifestyle of strength, and a confident security better observed than discussed, participated in rather than talked about. When a man gives of himself, lays his life down, and positions himself as an instrument of redemption, he is taking up his God-ordained station in life.

Men provide life by giving their own life away. This is what those men have done who died for our country. When we walk past the war memorials in Washington, D.C., the reverence we give and the honor we feel is because we know their selfless service makes it possible for us to live our lives in peace. On a more routine basis, this is what a man does who gives his life by sharing it with those he loves, even if it is as simple as a walk beside Rocky Creek. The ability of another person to live as God intended for them is the reverence and honor given because we laid down our lives.

A strong man is a courageous man, and a courageous man takes on the responsibilities of life while depending upon his Heavenly Father. There is nothing more courageous or influential than a man who loves, prays, leads a disciplined life, encourages others, and serves as Christ served.

Love

Instead of languishing under the weight of shame left to us by Adam, we can cloak ourselves in the courage of Christ as the strong, secure men we are. This is the foundation equipping us to build a life of practical redemption for those closest to us. A courageous man *loves,* not because those he loves perform like he wants them to, but because of who he is and who they are. He loves because he is a loving person and because they need his love. And, he loves because love Himself lives in him.

Prayer

A courageous man is a man of *prayer.* But before you conjure up an image of yourself kneeling in your closet for an hour, you need to know a courageous man of prayer communicates with his Father while doing what he needs to do, never dropping his guard against the insidious enemy he faces.

The Scripture says we are to pray without ceasing. This can only mean God intends prayer to occur in all venues of life: kneeling, lying down, eating, riding, walking, running, working, loving, caring, kissing the kids good night, going to the ball game, or fishing (although I must admit, I pray all the time when I'm fishing and it doesn't do any good).

Prayer is doing with God what He has already done with you. God has shared everything He has with you, all of His hopes, dreams, aspirations, convictions, disappointments, hurts, and even the life of His eldest son, in anticipation of your responding at the same level. Courageous prayer is communicating with your Father in a similar fashion and taking those closest to you on your journey toward His heart. As you communicate with them from your heart, and let them observe you doing the same with your Father, they see a model of the relationship you have with Him through your communication with them and your communication with God.

A Disciplined Life

A courageous man lives a *disciplined life* that demonstrates the important elements of life and transfers those priorities to those within his sphere of influence. A disciplined life is a life with structure and parameters. Please don't hear me talking about rigidity or advocating the adoption of standards that squelch spontaneity. Actually, it is discipline that creates the fertile soil where creativity, spontaneity, and the courage to look at life in a unique way flourishes most readily. An undisciplined life breeds insecurity and wastes time, a precious commodity. A courageous man disciplines his life according to his Father's priorities.

I mustn't leave this point without exhorting you to guard yourself and those you love against legalism disguised as discipline. Legalism is all about control, performance-based acceptance, and rules devised by insecure folks who are threatened by the uniqueness of the human spirit and the profound grace of God. Discipline, on the other hand, sets us free to follow our Father's lead and examine all He has in store for us. The security offered by legalism is a limited perspective looking through a well-defined key-hole. The security of a disciplined lifestyle rests in the strong arms of our Father, and views the broad horizon of life from heaven's reaches. The difficulty in distinguishing between legalism and discipline often arises because both legalism and discipline can be preached from God's Word. However, knowing your Father's heart provides the discernment necessary to distinguish legalism from discipline. It is a timid soul who puts himself and God in a legalistic box to maintain the status quo. A courageous man views himself and his life from God's perspective and steps into the future with the discipline of a well-anchored, confident, and secure man.

Encouragement

I implore you, trust Christ, depend upon your Father, live life in this vibrant relationship, and *encourage* others to follow your lead. When Paul says to his readers in 1 Corinthians 11:1, "Be imitators of me," he wasn't being arrogant. He was being realistic. People are going to follow, to imitate, and they are going to model themselves after influential leaders. These titles include: dad, granddad, husband, friend, and mentor, and are all titles bestowing some degree of leadership, and therefore some degree of responsibility. If you are the bearer of any of these titles, you are expected to lead, not in the same way a sergeant leads, but through your lifestyle.

If you are a man, you are expected to be anchored. When strength is needed, a man is expected to be strong. Accepting this responsibility is not arrogance but necessity. Encouraging your kids, your friends, your colleagues, your wife, and those around you to follow your lead in life as you follow Christ's lead means you are acting like a strong man. It might be good to remember 1 Corinthians 16:13: "Be on the alert, stand firm in the faith, act like men, be strong."

This doesn't mean you stand up on your desk at work and take charge, or announce at the dinner table that you are the boss and have it all under control. We lead by example. Lead through love, communication, discipline, and encouragement emanating from your warrior heart—a heart committed to your Father's cause. A courageous man leads and encourages by taking his little girl's hand, his boy's shoulder, or his wife's arm. It is courageous leadership when a man stands beside his friend who has lost everything he held dear in order that he might be encouraged toward the One who is most dear.

Service

A courageous man *serves* from a heart in tune with his Father's heart. The life of Christ will only become meaningful as you demonstrate it by allowing Him to live His life through you. We are all imitators and we are all leaders. We already know the importance of having trusted men stand with us in life, but we must also make those closest to us part of our lives, choosing to stand by them.

In his book about fathers and sons, Bill Hanson tells about the relationship he has with his young son, Miles:

> If I am mowing the lawn, Miles mows the lawn also. If I am reading the paper, Miles reads the paper. If I am thirsty, so is Miles. Amazing, but he is imitating my steps as I once copied my own father's. Here is the cycle of life. We learn from our fathers, so we can teach our children.[85]

Being a servant is not a meek, mild job. It is the job of a warrior, and it requires great courage. A servant who serves by choice is secure in his identity and source. As a matter of fact, he is secure enough to lay his life down on behalf of another. Jesus Christ was the most courageous, strong man who ever lived, but His strength was not only exhibited when He drove the money changers out of the temple. It was also demonstrated when he went to bat for the woman caught in adultery, invited Himself to Zaccheus' home for dinner, stopped to find out who touched His robe in search of healing, and offered redemption to his friend, Peter, who had failed him miserably.

Being a dad is only one of the arenas where men are called upon to handle themselves courageously. Let me share a letter that came to our office recently written by a loving father:

Being masculine means holding my 5-year-old daughter, protecting her from the lightning while reading her favorite story for the hundredth time. Or camping with my 10-year-old boy and explaining why God designed the bark on a tree for its protection, and how He cared enough about us for that same tree to die so we can enjoy the fire we now have to cook our food. In other words, masculinity is spending time with our children. Kids will long forget the prizes or gifts we give them before the memories of the time we spent with them fade away.[86]

Brother, you can do these things and adopt these roles because you are secure in Christ. Make yourself vulnerable, share your heart, be transparent, for you are anchored deeply enough to withstand whatever comes your way.

But I must remind you, you won't accomplish these things by resolving to try harder or promising to do better. Remember, that is not the Father's plan. He intends for you to depend upon Him as your source. Doing otherwise is walking after the flesh and disappointing to your Father, not to mention a bad example of masculinity. Trusting your Father is not an arrangement of convenience—if you intend to find satisfaction in your heart and fulfillment in your masculinity, depending upon your Father must be your lifestyle. As C.S. Lewis writes, "Christ says, 'Give me all. I don't want so much of your time and so much of your money and so much of your work: I want you.'"[87]

LEADERSHIP ISN'T OPTIONAL

23

I like what Pastor E.V. Hill said in one of his sermons: "A man may call himself a leader, but if there isn't anyone following he's merely taking a walk." You may not be the chairman of a Fortune 500 company, but you have followers. They may be scattered all over creation for a variety of reasons, but you have followers. You may have undermined their trust in you as a leader, but they are nevertheless followers of you. Who are these people? Your wife, your kids, the people in the neighborhood and at your church, your friends, your colleagues, your business partner, your employees, your vendors, the folks you sit next to most Sundays, and the ladies at the day care. Think of the people who watch you for a statement about how to live. These are your followers.

Obviously, followers come in all shapes and sizes and are both distant and close, intimate and casual. To varying degrees, you and I have a responsibility to reflect masculinity to them. A real man lives his life the same way Jesus Christ lived His. He depends upon his Heavenly Father for his strength and is secure in the identity given to him by his Father. He lives the life of a redeemer—synonymous with a warrior—and lays his life down as a living sacrifice. The apostle Paul described real men in Philippians 2:5-8:

> Have this attitude in yourselves which was also in Christ Jesus, who, although He existed in the form of God, did not regard equality with God a thing to be grasped, but emptied Himself, taking the form of a bond-servant, and being made in the likeness of men. And being found in appearance as a man, He humbled Himself by becoming obedient to the point of death, even death on a cross.

To put it candidly, when we behave like men are supposed to behave, we show those looking in our direction a vision of Christ. The dad who loves his son and takes him through life depending upon his Heavenly Father is giving that son a living portrait of what God is like.

Effective Leaders Listen

Leaders are people who *listen* to discern what those around them are saying. If we do not hear what is said to us, our leadership will be impertinent. Before a leader can address the issues with words or actions he must hear and understand what the issues are. A speech irrelevant to life is at best an eloquent diversion, and at worst a waste of time. A speech answering the questions of life is more profound than a sermon—it is a message! And if spoken by a man depending upon his Heavenly Father, it is a message from God.

Effective Leaders Have Vision

A leader is a man of *vision*. Quite simply, he is a man whose feet are grounded, anchored in Christ, and whose eyes are scanning the horizon watching for his Heavenly Father's lead. A leader charts a course, navigates difficult places, and sets an example. He communicates his life by caring, teaching, encouraging, and persuading those he is leading to follow in his footsteps and emulate his lifestyle. And where are the footsteps and life of a secure man leading? Toward the Father.

An insecure man is self-absorbed, inward-looking, and cast down. Following such a man is like walking a snake's trail. Sooner or later you are going to find yourself lost, looking under rocks to regain your bearings.

This does not imply life will be faultless and trouble-free if men lead as God intended. Quite the contrary—warriors do not live in hot-houses and make their living tending the grounds. The purpose of a warrior is to advance, to protect, to defend, and to provide security. Walk with a warrior and you walk in enemy territory. But warriors do not simply walk, they march. They are secure in who they are and what they are to accomplish. They are confident in their King, their cause, their call, and in the good men who march beside them. I remind you: A man's security is in Christ and with other men.

Effective Leaders Are Passionate

A woman's job is to nurture and comfort, and this role is of vital importance. However, a man's job is to live life with *passion* and propagate a race of people who are strong because they know God and walk like Jesus walked. Alexander the Great's army was not successful because they held each other's hands, they were conquerors because they entrusted their lives into each other's hands and guarded one another's weaknesses in difficulty. They were not successful because Alexander was a great warrior who did all the fighting while they cheered from the sidelines. Every man went into battle and took the man next to him with him. They had a passion for their role, their task, and their partners.

Effective Leaders Are Facilitators

Leaders do not shelter those they care for from the harsh realities of life. They *facilitate* the ability of others to live passionate lives. Leaders do not bear their pain by themselves. They take those who are following them through the tumult—this is the only way those who follow will taste victory for themselves. Leaders do not deprive those they love from difficulty, but neither do leaders leave those they love in the storm by themselves. They don't let friends go into battle alone. Isn't this indicative of what our Father said to us in His blessing? We have always been on the road to victory together.

Effective Leaders Empower

Finally, leaders *empower* those who follow them to appropriate Christ's strength for themselves. This will occur as you talk with them, share your struggles with them, convey your convictions, declare your doubts, and tell them about the difficulties you are experiencing. Discuss how you are dealing with the challenge you are facing. Model how a man exhibits manhood. If you do not pass these skills to them, they will be in grave danger of being lost at sea when the storms of life rage against them.

Don't be naïve, leaders come in all shapes and sizes. People often equate leadership with charisma or flamboyance, but such is not the case. During World War II, two generals on the European front were known for their flair, ego, and strong personality: British field marshal Bernard "Monty" Montgomery and the American general George S. Patton. Both were successful, aggressive leaders who were instrumental in the allied victory over the Nazis and the Axis powers. However, behind them both was the calm, collected, almost boring, American general Dwight David Eisenhower.

In contrast to Patton's pearl-handled pistols and knee-high jack boots, "Ike" dressed in standard Army issue clothing. While both Montgomery and Patton commanded significant military contingents, Eisenhower commanded them as the supreme allied commander in Europe.

What set Eisenhower above Montgomery and Patton? In one sense, it was his lack of charisma, his lack of ego, his lack of flamboyance. He was predictable, consistent, slow to speak, and compassionate. These qualities invited people's trust and enabled great leadership to flourish. When coupled with the excellent training the allied troops received and the compelling vision of defeating the Nazis, the methodical leadership of Eisenhower promoted loyalty, trust, and self-sacrifice for the cause.

Leadership isn't about strutting your stuff, demanding allegiance, or drawing attention to yourself. The highest form of leadership comes from the man who steadily exhibits the fundamentals: listening, vision, passion, and facilitation and empowerment of others. Whether leading the board meeting or leading in prayer before bedtime, the man who accepts his responsibility as leader takes those following his lead into the honorable world of manhood.

24

THE DEFINING MOMENT

Coming to grips with the fact his dad had failed and dropped the ball wasn't the big issue for Martin Jacobson, the young man I was talking with over lunch. What he really wanted to know was, why his dad wouldn't "pick up the doggone ball."

Martin and I talked a few minutes over lunch and then made plans to get together and ride our mountain bikes on the rugged trails following the shoreline of Lake Grapevine north of the Dallas-Fort Worth Airport.

It was a fantastic day to ride. Both of us had taken off work mid-week, so we had the lake and the trails to ourselves. There was a light breeze, 80 degrees, and not a cloud in the sky. We rode hard, bobbing and weaving through the oak woods, dipping and diving through gullies and washes, climbing and digging our way up and over the sharp hills containing the lake. Hopping tree roots, dodging rocks, kicking up dust, and sucking air we looped back on ourselves and retraced our route back to the truck and a welcome dive into the lake.

Martin and I washed off the sweat and dirt from our ninety-minute ride, and hopefully the oil from any poison ivy we had brushed against. We loaded the bikes on the bicycle rack, then

dropped the tailgate of the truck to horizontal and sat looking at
the rippled waters of the lake showing off their garish diamonds
given them by the sun.

We retraced our conversational steps since we'd first talked
over lunch, and I listened as Martin not only recounted our conversation but talked of his subsequent insights. "So a man is like
a corner post, anchored in Christ, depending on his Heavenly
Father, and setting the standard against which everyone around
him pushes, pulls, strains, and gains bearing. You know, Pres, I
don't feel like I understand this very well yet, and I know I'm
going to have to think about it and pray about it some more, but
it feels right. There is something inside, a compulsion of some
sort I suppose, saying, 'Yes! I know this is who I am. And what I
want to be.'"

A Man's Station

Men aren't born, nor does a boy just become a man somewhere between puberty and adulthood. Men are *formed*. While a
boy may grow to look like a man, his sense of masculinity is tied
to the influence of an older man. And while a girl will grow to
look like a woman, hopefully gaining a sense of femininity from
her mother, the role of a man in her successful arrival at womanhood is undeniable.

A man's station in life is to position himself as an instrument
of redemption, laying his life down so others may truly live as
God intended them to live. He takes his place as a corner post.

From where he is stationed, a man can see the great war
raging between the evil forces of Satan and the godly forces of his
Father. Ebbing and waning around him, he knows his only hope
for victory resides in his Father, and that his security is in Christ
and the trusted men at his side. In his heart a man knows he has
the resource to shift the battle's momentum in his Father's direction, but he must act like a man and be strong.

Not only must a man be strong in his Father's strength, he must pass this quality of strength to others, primarily those younger ones under his influence, especially his sons and daughters. They must recognize God as their source of sufficiency and find their significance and security in Him. They must come to know Him as more than the God of the man they admire; they must know Him and depend upon Him as their Father. The man who is blessed by his Father—which you are—knows the pivotal role he plays in facilitating this process and perpetuating this blessing.

A man like Martin does not have to grieve over the fumbled blessing from a man who failed in his task. He is blessed by God, his Heavenly Father. When a man blesses those he loves, he is speaking on God's behalf and verbalizing what is on His heart. Perhaps the moments when our masculinity is exhibited most convincingly are those moments when we bless those in our care. When we bless, we speak for God. Real leaders do not delegate the one thing they can do with excellence better than anyone else. Men who are leaders *bless* their families as an act of redemption.

The Blessing: Preparation

Everyone within your sphere of influence needs your blessing. Not only is it their need, but it is your responsibility and privilege as a man to give it. Your role is not just essential, it is indispensable. Only a man can provide a man's blessing. Since this book is primarily written to discuss masculinity, I will discuss blessing from the perspective of a father blessing his son. But this should in no way diminish your commitment to generalize from what is to follow and bless your daughter. If there are young men besides your son looking to you as their primary masculine role model, don't forget to hand the ball to them with a definitive, secure blessing as well. Finally, your wife can be involved in blessing your kids, but only you can provide a man's blessing, since you are the corner post they are looking toward. Be strong, act like a man, depend on your Father, and bless them. Now is not a good time for a fumble.

Just like you needed to hear your Father speak His blessing and acceptance to you, your son needs to hear you bless him. By giving your blessing and acceptance to him, you position your son to receive his Father's blessing and acceptance. In blessing him, you position your son for the transition from boyhood—dependence upon you—to manhood—dependence upon his Heavenly Father.

A boy never gets too old to receive his father's blessing. It is not uncommon for me to end a men's conference with a time of blessing where I verbalize our Father's words to the men who need to be blessed. I ask any man in the audience who failed to receive his dad's blessing to stand up. Men of all shapes, sizes, and ages readily stand to their feet, to be joined by their brothers who come to stand beside them in their time of honesty and vulnerability. There are many bald-headed, wrinkled, old men who feel like insecure boys because they never received a definitive blessing from their dad signaling they had made it to manhood.

Brother, the boy you need to bless and welcome into manhood may have boys of his own who are past due receiving their blessing from him. Remember the words of Martin Jacobsen concerning his dad. If your responsibility to bless your son has been fumbled, pick up the ball and prepare to hand it off.

I am an advocate of creating a rite of passage that defines very clearly a fundamental change has occurred. There has been an irreversible transition—from this point forward, things will never be the same again. A boy has become a man with all the rights, responsibilities, and privileges associated with manhood. Part of blessing is making this a reality. Of course, you must be convinced about the validity of what you are doing. While we men didn't get our fair share of intuition, we can usually tell if someone is just blowing hot air. Don't try to pass a half-baked, half-hearted, half-witted blessing off on your son. He won't buy it. With your blessing, be prepared to make things different as soon as you stand up to leave the room. You must treat your son like who he is—a man—instead of who you feel like he is and who you have known him to be all of his life—your boy. Define the new role your son is stepping into and talk to him about the new game plan. Ease his mind about the insecurity he feels, and reassure him by explaining what you know about security.

In their book, *The Gift of the Blessing,* Gary Smalley and John Trent teach that a blessing is unconditional and eternal, and should be delivered with a meaningful touch and spoken words. It should express high value, picture a special future, and include an active commitment to the blessing given.[88] They say this about all blessings—which they believe should occur frequently—not just the one-time, formal rite of blessing I am preparing to describe. I agree with them. Frequent blessing should be a normal, routine part of a man's life. Coupled with a hug or a pat or a bump or a kiss, these words communicate your unconditional acceptance and pride in them.

However, I am making a distinction between routine blessing and the blessing that is a rite of passage from boyhood to manhood. The blessing I am talking about contains all the elements of a routine blessing, but it is a formal declaration happening one time and then remaining as a point of reference. In other words, there can be many experiences of blessing, but only one blessing marking the passage into manhood. You should regularly bless your ten-year-old son, but you should not transfer the mantle of masculinity to him.

This brings up a good question: When should you bless your son with his rite of passage into manhood? Given our current culture, I think the age range from 17–23 is an appropriate window. There will be some young men who are ready at 18, as they graduate high school, and others who aren't yet mature enough for your blessing to be meaningful. Circumstances may dictate the timing of your blessing more than your son's maturity. For example, if your son is preparing to leave school and join the armed forces, now is a good time to give your blessing.

By the time a young man is graduating college, he probably needs to hear your blessing even if you don't think he is ready. There is no sacred or magical time. Without a doubt, the most important element of your blessing is performing the blessing man to man, then working diligently to back up your blessing with your actions.

If you missed your opportunity and your son is out from under your roof, now is the time to begin working toward this event. He is not too old for you to bless him—Jacob was probably 40 years old when Isaac blessed him. You may need to include a sincere apology to your son for dropping the ball, but it is never too late to bless and it is never so awkward it should not be carried out. Martin Jacobsen wasn't confused with why his dad dropped the ball, but with why he didn't pick it up. Pick the ball up, brother. The quicker you correct course, the more chance you have of strengthening your relationship.

In addition to the elements mentioned earlier, the blessing for a rite of passage should be done at a formal time and place, there should be a formal declaration, and there should be a formal commemoration of the passage from boyhood to manhood.

Plan a Formal Time and Place

Think this through ahead of time. You are going to have a personal, intimate discussion with your son. Emotion will be high and the situation may feel awkward. It would be a shame to have the waitress ask, "More tea, sir?" just as you are about to speak the climax of your blessing to your boy. The same could be said for your beeper going off, your cell phone ringing, or your youngest bursting through the door to ask if Jerry can spend the night in the tent. Eliminate the chance for interruption like you did the night you asked your wife to marry you. This is a big deal, and it is up to you to convey how big of a deal it is by how you plan the occasion.

You may choose to go to dinner first, then to a place where you can talk privately. You may go on a camping trip together, a fishing trip, or a weekend with a ball game, golfing, and overnight in a nice hotel. You may include the family if they are all old enough to respect what is occurring, or you may choose to have a reception. This is your big chance to say what you need to say and do what you need to do so that your son gets the message. Don't read the last page of this book and yell for your son to come out to the garage with you so you can "talk about something for a minute" while you're sharpening the lawnmower blade. Plan a formal time and place.

Prepare a Formal Declaration

Decide ahead of time what you are going to say to your son. Write it down and read it, or at least speak from a detailed outline. If your son is far away, I would advise against writing something and giving it to your son to read on his own. If need be, write it down, read it onto a tape recorder, and then send the letter and the tape together to him. Now is not the time for an impromptu speech, jokes, or comments off the cuff. Neither is this a roast. It is a formal occasion.

Your son needs to hear you speak your words with your own mouth, and ideally he needs to see you work your way through this blessing of passage. It doesn't matter how hard it is to get through this, what matters most is that you get through it and he sees you do it and knows you did it for him. You are laying your life down, putting your heart on the table, and doing what is best for him. This is an act of redemption. In this sense, you are exemplifying through your life what your Father has done—this is a portrait your son cannot afford to miss seeing. This is one of the biggest games of your career, so standing on the sidelines because you feel inhibited and embarrassed, or botching the hand off because you didn't prepare ahead of time, is the rough equivalent of dropping the ball. You know how your Heavenly Father handed the ball to you, now it is time for you to depend upon Him and follow His lead with your son.

Plan a Formal Commemoration

Commemorations, celebrations, and consecrations of this sort are best memorialized with a gift. As you will see in the sample blessing that follows, I give a fly rod and reel as a commemoration of the mantle of manhood being passed. Your gift could be almost anything of lasting value to both you and your son: a watch, a ring, a knife, a plaque, a gun, a picture, a classic writing pen, or something else of similar significance, longevity, and value. The gift should not be something like a car, a new pair of shoes, a suit, college tuition, a down payment, or cash. While these are fine gifts, they are either temporal or something you were going to provide anyway. Instead, you are looking for something extraordinary to give him, something he can hold in his hands that will have intrinsic value to him forty years from now because it came from you on the occasion of his passage from boyhood to manhood. The gift you give is to commemorate for him the day he was declared a man, welcomed into the world of men by his father.

Creating a Defining Moment

What you are about to read is a template. If need be, use my words as your own with your son. However, don't feel compelled to speak your blessing like I would. Take the elements of my words and speak from your heart. God bless you, brother. I'm beside you in this, and of course, your Heavenly Father is proud of your commitment to assume your station in life. With these words you create a defining moment:

> This is a significant moment for me, a momentous occasion, and a defining moment for you. Ever since you were born I've known in my heart this day would come. And now, here it is, one of those points in time that defines life, makes it worth living, and allows us to touch the future.

> This day has been in the making since the doctor placed you into my arms—what seems like only a few moments ago. I guess it is true time flies when you are having fun, and what a grand time I have had participating in your journey from childhood to manhood.

> I have some things I want to say to you, and I believe with all my heart I am not only speaking for myself, but also for the One whom I serve and whom I have tried to point you toward: the King of kings and Lord of lords, my Heavenly Father.

> I am proud of you, and certainly I could list a number of accomplishments on the ledger beside your name. But while I am immensely proud of those things, on a more fundamental basis, I'm proud of *you*. I'm proud of who you are and the person you have become. I'm proud of the character etched deep inside you, making you the person you are. I'm proud of the passion you have for people and for life. Were you suddenly to lose all of your ability to do anything, I would still be proud of you. What makes me proud is what is buried deep inside your soul, making you, you. I'm proud of you, son.

> I also have confidence in you. I believe in you. Regardless of what you choose to do in life, the world would be a poorer place without you. I believe you are a person worthy of my trust and confidence, not that you will always perform perfectly, but I have confidence in the basic tenets that make

you the person you are. I trust you as a person I would like to have as my friend, my companion, my colleague.

There is part of me that would love the opportunity to do some things over again. I have made mistakes that have hurt you and that I'm ashamed of. With more frequency than I like to admit, I have walked after my old ways, and in so doing, have not exemplified before you the person I truly am and aspire to convey. I want you to know I am sorry for the ways I have dropped the ball in your life. By God's grace, and as He gives me insight, my determination is to pick up the fumbles and carry the responsibilities He has given me with more diligence. But I do ask you to hear my heart and forgive me.

On the other hand, as only God can do, He has taken my shortcomings and woven His plan to form a beautiful tapestry in your life. From the front, your life is a work of art, but when the tapestry of your life is turned over there are knots and strings and frayed ends. I know there is a temptation to clip the ends and pull on loose strings in an effort to make the back of the tapestry look as beautiful as the front, but in so doing, the tapestry begins to unravel, and it is only then you discover the frayed ends on the back have a beauty all their own and work together to make the tapestry strong. You are a beautiful person, a rich tapestry. I encourage you to let people see your beauty from both sides and don't tolerate anyone who discounts you because you are a unique individual. As imperfect as it may seem to you, God has made you a beautiful person, and one I count myself privileged to know and love.

You now have the opportunity and responsibility to trust Christ for every aspect of your life and depend upon your Heavenly Father to be your source, sufficiency, and security. Herein lies the great secret to strength.

From the day I knew you were conceived, I loved you. I was proud you were mine. I passed out cigars to anyone who would stop long enough to listen the day you were born. My buddies congratulated me, and hugged me, and proposed toasts to you and me: "Here's to an inseparable team. May you transfer to this boy enough of yourself to create a legacy, and enough of your heart to make him great. And may he grow to be twice the man you are and aspire to be. Hear, hear!"

I have admired you from the day you began on your stumbling, toddling trek to this day. As you walked in this evening, I admired your confidence and the manner in which you carry yourself. You have made me proud and I am honored to be here with you at this moment.

Now, a milestone has appeared in the path. The day has come for you to pass from being a boy to being a man. As your dad, I'm here today to declare this momentous occasion has occurred and to give you my blessing. You are no longer a boy. Today you are a man, unconditionally worthy to shoulder all of the responsibility, and share in all the joys, that come with manhood. Congratulations, you have made it. The milestone is behind you and the world of manhood is before you.

I will always be your dad and you will always be my son, but today you are no longer my boy. Today, you have become a man, my peer. I will no longer treat you as a boy. Instead, I will treat you as a partner and friend with all of the position, authority, and respect manhood deserves.

You have passed from depending on me as your dad to a position of full responsibility as a man. Now your dependence must be upon your Heavenly Father. Just as you have looked to me for identity, meaning, and worth, you must now look to Him, not me, not the things of this world, not those around you, but to Him. He is the source and secret of true strength, significance, and security. These are things only men know.

From one man to another, I exhort you to take up your station in life. Anchor yourself in Christ. Pursue knowing your

Heavenly Father. Lean on Him and share everything in life with Him. Do not isolate yourself. Always keep watch for godly men you can build close relationships with, who will help you remain true to the One whose name you bear and who blesses you along with me today.

Deep within you there is a vault, cared for by the Spirit of God Himself. Stored in that treasure house is everything you need to trust Christ, love your Heavenly Father, care for the people around you, and live life. May your future be rich with all of the affluence available to you through investing the treasure in the vault. May you always walk with a determined step, Christ-like character, unswerving integrity, and may your head be held high with the confidence of one who knows he is a strong man. Finally, when you reach the end of your life's journey, may you say with conviction, "I have run a good race, fought a good fight, lived life with passion, and loved my Heavenly Father with all my heart. And in my final days, if God will supply His grace, I will trust Him to let my legacy live beyond me."

God never intended you to walk alone. I would love to be one of those men you consider to be your friend. And today I would like to invite you to be one of the men in my life— a friend along with Joe, Randy, Ed, and Jared.

As a symbol of this defining moment, I have purchased something for you I intend to be in your heart forever and in your hand regularly until you depart from this planet. The enemy of God will try everything within his power to divert you from your responsibility and position as a man who is depending upon his Heavenly Father. This Sage #6-weight fly rod and Orvis fly reel will always remind you that both your Heavenly Father and your earthly father have deemed you worthy to bear the title, "A Real Man."

I love you son, and I am now—in this defining moment— proud to count you as my friend.

THINGS ONLY HEROES KNOW

25

A man's story is the classic tale of the struggle between good and evil. As is the case in any story, there must be a hero, one who appears to be facing odds beyond his ability to overcome, and yet one who prevails. A man recognizes the formidable foe he faces on the spiritual battlegrounds of life and determines for the good of those who follow in his footsteps to take up the fight against the Prince of Darkness who wages war against his Father, the God of the Universe. The enemy's strategy is to deaden the resonance of masculinity in the hearts of men so they will no longer portray an accurate representation of their Father and thus discredit Him and themselves.

But a man knows his strength is not shown through the world's means, but demonstrated by depending upon his Heavenly Father, a lesson he has known from the day he was born. He knows his source for victory is not resident in his own soul, but endowed upon him by his Father's sufficiency.

A man knows the significance of his manhood is not based upon his competency, worth, or achievement, but upon the solid fact he is anchored in Christ as a corner post. His Father paid the price to have him as His friend. A man's security is in the fact that his elder Brother has been commissioned by the Father to stand with him, and He has brought strong men to stand alongside His younger brother.

But this is not all that makes a man. A real man knows his station in life is one of redemption. That is the role the one, true man, Jesus Christ, exemplified and intends for men to emulate through His power. The first man, Adam, had an opportunity to lay his life down and failed. The last man, Jesus Christ, picked up Adam's dropped ball and offered Himself as an instrument of redemption.

A man knows in his heart these same choices await his decision. Will he follow in the footsteps of his forefather, Adam, or station himself as an instrument of redemption, a warrior engaged in a noble cause, willing to lay down his life so others may live as his Father intended? A man knows in his heart that masculinity is a life of redemption.

And now a toast to you: *Here's to my brothers, my comrades in arms, heroes every one. May you march on the road to victory a strong man and a courageous warrior, among other strong men and courageous warriors, and may you bless those who come after you. Hear, hear!*

1. Barbara Kantrowitz and Claudia Kalb, "Boys Will Be Boys," *Newsweek*, May 11, 1998, p.56.

2. Robert Bly, *Iron John* (Reading, Massachusetts: Addison-Wesley Publishing Company, Inc., 1990), p.2.

3. Ibid., p.23.

4. Dr. James Dobson, *Straight Talk* (Dallas, Texas: Word Publishing, 1991), p.23.

5. Jack Hayford, *A Man's Starting Place* (Van Nuys, CA: Living Way Ministries, 1992), p.21.

6. Dr. James Dobson, p.33.

7. Sally Quinn, "Who Killed Feminism?" *Washington Post,* January 11, 1992, C1, Col. 1.

8. Ibid.

9. Ibid.

10. Ibid., C2, Col. 1.

11. Ibid.

12. John Gray, *Men Are from Mars, Women Are from Venus* (New York, NY: HarperCollins Publishers, Inc., 1992), p.31.

13. Gail Sheehy, "How (And How Not) to Age Well," *Parade*, April 26, 1998, p.4.

14. Robert Bly, p.60.

15. Grant Wahl and L. John Wertheim, "Paternity Ward," *Sports Illustrated,* May 4, 1998, p.70.

16. Gordon MacDonald, *When Men Think Private Thoughts* (Nashville, TN: Thomas Nelson Publishers, 1996), p. 17.

17. Ralph Waldo Emerson, "Self-Reliance," Carl Bode, ed., *The Portable Emerson* (New York, NY: Viking Penguin, 1946), p. 139.

18. William Ernest Henley, "Invictus," *One Hundred and One Famous Poems* (Chicago, IL: The Reilly & Lee Co., 1958), p. 95.

19. Stu Weber, *Tender Warrior* (Sisters, OR: Multnomah Books, 1993), p. 172.

20. See Philippians 4:13.

21. See Romans 5:12-19.

22. Jack Hayford, p. 75.

23. See Ephesians 5:25-32.

24. Jack Hayford, pp. 24-25.

25. See Romans 5:12ff.

26. Hebrews 10:16.

27. Gary Smalley and Dr. John Trent, *The Hidden Value of a Man* (Colorado Springs, CO: Focus on the Family Publishing, 1992), p. 92.

28. Jack Hayford, pp. 60-61.

29. Ibid., pp. 61-62.

30. Gary Smalley and Dr. John Trent, p. 147.

31. Robert Bly, p. 16.

32. See Hebrews 11:32-34.

33. Robert Bly, p. ix.

34. Skip Hamilton, "Group Therapy: Paceline Riding De-mystified," *Bicycling,* May 1997, p. 94.

35. Ken Gire, *Windows of the Soul* (Grand Rapids, MI: Zondervan Publishing House, 1996), p. 76.

36. Used by permission: Frank Perkins, "Christmas gift treasured 46 years later," *Fort Worth Star-Telegram,* Friday, December 25, 1992, Section A, p. 1.

37. Roger Rosenblatt, "One on One," *Family Circle,* July 21, 1992, p. 182.

38. Robert Bly, pp. 15-16.

39. Norman Maclean, *A River Runs Through It* (Chicago, IL: The University of Chicago Press, 1976), p. 1.

40. See 1 Corinthians 6:20.

41. Jack Hayford, *A Man's Image and Identity* (Van Nuys, CA: Living Way Ministries, 1993), p. 27.

42. See Romans 5:12-19.

43. Calvin Miller, "I Know Men," *Home Life,* March 1997, p. 53.

44. C.S. Lewis, "The Necessity of Chivalry," Walter Hooper, ed., *Present Concerns: Essays by C.S. Lewis* (New York, NY: Harcourt Brace Jovanovich, Publishers, 1986), p. 13.

45. Robert Bly, p. 42.

46. Ralph Waldo Emerson, p. 139.

47. See Psalm 56:8.

48. Compiled from Psalms 33:17; 46:1; 59:16; 73:26; 105:4; 118:14; 147:10; 28:7.

49. Note: An ephod was a linen apron used in praying.

50. For more on this, see Henri J.M. Nouwen, *The Return of the Prodigal Son* (New York, NY: Image Books, Bantam Doubleday Dell Publishing Group, Inc., 1992), p. 82.

51. See Romans 6:1-11 and Galatians 2:20.

52. For an interesting discussion of this see Romans 7:14-25 and Bill Gillham's book, *Lifetime Guarantee* (Eugene, OR: Harvest House Publishers, 1993), Chapter 6, pp. 101-118.

53. Note: This statement is not intended to lend credence to the perverted theological notion of sinless perfection. No one can experience sinless perfection. Only one man, Jesus Christ, lived a sinless life. However, as believers—regenerate men—we are free from the irresistible compulsion we had as lost men to sin and are compelled from within our new heart and the indwelling Holy Spirit to walk in obedience to our Father, God. See Romans 5:12–6:23 specifically and Romans 5–8 in a broader context.

54. See Matthew 25:41.

55. See Ephesians 6:10-20.

56. See Romans 6:12.

57. See Philippians 4:8.

58. This story is compiled from: Exodus 17:8-16, Deuteronomy 25:17-18, Genesis 36:12, 12:12, 25:27-34, and Malachi 1:3.

59. Major W. Ian Thomas, *The Saving Life of Christ* (Grand Rapids, MI: Zondervan Publishing Co., 1961), p. 93.

60. Ibid., p. 88.

61. See 1 Samuel 15:1-35; 28:15-19.

62. For example, see Deuteronomy 32:18; 2 Samuel 22:3; Psalm 18:2; Isaiah 17:10; 1 Corinthians 10:4.

63. Mike Yorkey and Peb Jackson, "Finding New Friends on the Block," *Focus on the Family,* June 1992, p. 3.

64. Stu Weber, p. 172.

65. Reference: Matthew 26:36-46.

66. Patrick M. Morley, *The Man in the Mirror* (Brentwood, TN: Wolgemuth & Hyatt, Publisher, Inc., 1989), p. 117.

67. C.S. Lewis, *The Four Loves* (New York, NY: Harcourt Brace Jovanovich, 1960), p. 104.

68. Stu Weber, *Locking Arms* (Sisters, OR: Multnomah Books, 1995), p. 155.

69. Ibid., p. 81.

70. Ibid., p. 88.

71. Max Falls, personal fax to the author, November 25, 1996.

72. C.S. Lewis, *The Four Loves,* pp. 126-127.

73. Used by permission.

74. Peter F. Drucker, *The Effective Executive* (New York, NY: Harper & Row, Publishers, 1966), p. 173.

75. See Philippians 4:19.

76. See Romans 6:11-12.

77. Elisabeth Elliot, *Shadow of the Almighty: The Life and Testament of Jim Elliot* (New York, NY: Harper Brothers Publishers, 1958), p. 247.

78. See Isaiah 14:12ff.

79. See Matthew 26:69-75; Mark 14:66-72; Luke 22:55-62; John 18:16-18, 25-27.

80. See 1 Corinthians 3:10-15.

81. Theodore Roosevelt, "The Strenuous Life," 10 April 1899, Houston Peterson, ed., *A Treasury of the World's Great Speeches* (New York, NY: Simon and Schuster, 1954), p. 656.

82. See Philippians 4:8; Colossians 3:2 et al.

83. For a broader discussion of this subject, I encourage you to read Bill Gillham's book *Lifetime Guarantee*, published by Harvest House Publishers, 1993.

84. Note: For more information on this step in the recovery process, I encourage you to contact our office for a copy of the booklet *A Study of the Mind*. We have a multiplicity of material on this subject, and closely related subjects, since this is one of the primary foci of our ministry.

85. Bill Hanson, *Father and Son: The Bond* (Austin, TX: Bright Books, 1996), p. 2.

86. Used by permission. Letter on file with the author.

87. C.S. Lewis, *Mere Christianity* (New York, NY: Macmillan Publishing Company, Inc., 1943), p. 167.

88. For further details, see Gary Smalley and John Trent, *The Gift of the Blessing* (Nashville, TN: Thomas Nelson Publishers, 1993), p. 173.